MW01292069

# BUILDING
# FINANCIAL FENCES

by
Mark Wagner

Copyright © 2016 by Dunhill Marketing
www.dunhillinsurance.com
All Rights Reserved.
ISBN: 978-1537572710
Printed in the United States of America
Cover Image: Allied Productions, Spring Valley, CA.

Inside Artwork: Special thanks to my nephew Samuel Wagner
Your talent is beginning to shine!

# TABLE OF CONTENTS

## Section 7: Long Term Care

## Section 8: Conclusions

# INTRODUCTION

# Chapter 1

# WE ARE ALL ON A JOURNEY

Every one of us is on a journey in life. Some aspects of the journey we all share in common. For instance, we can all point to the day we were born. We will all face the day when our earthly life comes to an end. We all grew up in a family, went to school, have had jobs along the way, experienced friendship and heartaches and have a place we call home. At the same time, many aspects of your journey are unique to you. The events of your life form a unique story of memories and lessons that have made you who you are today.

The same is true of your financial journey. You have a unique story of earning, investing and planning. Your financial plan will be most effective if it matches who you are as an individual, the season of life you find yourself in and the goals you have for your life. If these all line up, you will be financially effective and peaceful.

To help you identify the significant experiences of your journey, I would like to share with you the parts of my life that have had the biggest impact on me. They have shaped who I am, how I think and the approach I take to decisions in my life. I think you will find that we have some experiences in common. As you read those, I hope it will confirm the important conclusions that shape your approach to life. I think you will also discover that some of my story is different than yours. I hope you at least find those stories amusing and that they stimulate your thinking.

Let's jump in!

## Bold Beginnings

I was one of those kids who couldn't be ignored because I was energetic and outspoken. When I was 12 years old, I used to attend monthly men's business meetings at church with my dad. I would rather have gone fishing or played with my friends but my father insisted. So I attended the meetings and I took notes. My dad required me to take notes on all sermons which included these monthly meetings.

It was frustrating to me as a kid. It seemed to me that the same business would come up every month. They probably made more progress than I realized but to a young man it seemed we were covering the same topics every time. I actually said at one of the meetings, "If you gave these issues to the kids, we could solve them quickly and then we could all go fishing." The men just laughed and turned back to their conversation. Dad taught me and my siblings that kids were supposed to be silent so he just nodded at me and told me to keep taking notes.

One of the items that kept coming up for discussion was the need volunteers to preach at a sister church in Franklin, PA. It was about 55 miles away so it wasn't a convenient assignment. Our church was teaching boys how to speak, pray or read scripture in public so I was surprised that no one was taking up the challenge. After having heard this come up for discussion too many times, I decided to speak up. I accidentally knocked my chair over as I stood up and announced, "I will do it if someone will take me." A man in the back agreed to take me, the motion was seconded and I was "elected" to bring the message.

## Who You Are Counts!

It was an unforgettable experience, especially for the adults. I was short. Even today, I am just 5' 6" tall. I used to think being short made me different, even though I could do the same things as other people. I just had to work harder or approach the challenges differently. Learning to overcome obstacles became the secret of my success as a public speaker. People were amused because they had to put books on the floor for me to stand on so I could see over the pulpit. It must have gone okay because I was elected to speak again the next week and the next. Attendance grew with each message because it was entertaining to see the "little preacher" in action.

In the same way, there is something about you that makes you unique. It may be your height or your body type. It may be the pitch of your voice or the style of your hair. It may be a unique ability you possess. You may be proud of this unique characteristic or you may have been ridiculed for the same trait throughout your life. Either way, this unique characteristic may be the very thing that creates the greatest platform in your life for being productive and helpful to others.

## Questions Create Uncomfortable Confidence

After the first sermon, Brother Ham asked me follow up questions about my message. It was frustrating because I didn't have answers. I had studied and prepared the message but I didn't really understand the information. It felt like an interrogation even though Brother Ham's intention was to test me so I would grow. With a few pointed questions, he revealed to both of us that I wasn't quite prepared. After that first week, I was hoping Brother Ham wouldn't talk to me after my next message. It was just wishful thinking, however, much like hoping birds won't come to birdfeeder you have loaded with bird food. Every week, Brother Ham was relentless in asking questions.

I told mom, "He keeps asking me questions that I don't have answers to."

Mom told me, "Well, now that you know the questions, you can go find the answers."

That led me to do more diligent research so I wouldn't feel

ignorant around Brother Ham. It was a great life lesson for me. Being prepared as much as possible helped me perform better and helped me avoid embarrassing conversations. I preached as a fill-in throughout high school which raised my confidence level and gave an enjoyable outlet for my outgoing personality.

I have since learned this principle applies to much more than just preaching as a young man. I sure hope my doctor knows enough to answer my questions! I have always wanted my bosses to be able to answer questions not just give orders. My kids have always wanted me to address their questions not just give them my agenda. I am also keenly aware that my clients are hoping I can address their financial questions rather than just sell them products. Questions are your friends so keep asking and welcome those who are willing to ask you questions that make you uncomfortable!

## Looks Can Be Mighty Deceiving

As I mentioned, I have been short my whole life. I was the oldest in my family but you would never know it from looking at our family. Because of my size, I had to learn to adjust in ways other people didn't. For instance, I started bailing hay at 12. I was so short, however, that I couldn't reach the platform of the hay wagon. To buck the bales up and into place, I had to do it differently than all the other boys. I learned to bounce the bale off my knee and up into the air so I could balance it on my shoulders. From there I could push it up on the wagon as the tractor pulled past me. I had to be innovative because I had to keep up with the others since it was my summer job. At first, the local farmers didn't think I could keep up but they quickly learned that you can't tell a book by its cover.

## The Lunch Run

One day when I was in high school my younger brother forgot

his lunch. His bus left for school before mine did. Mom realized he had forgotten his lunch before my bus left so she asked me to deliver it. In our little town, our schools were about a half mile apart. In order to get to class on time, I ran from my school down to his, sprinted down the hallway to my brother's class and delivered the goods. After the successful mission, I reentered the hall and began racing for the exit so I could get back to my school. One of the school teacher's called after me and told me I couldn't run in the hall. She tried to stop me and send me back to my room at the middle school. I was so small she thought there was no way I could be in high school. It took all my persuasive skills to finally convince her that I was going to be late for my real class at the high school if she didn't let me go.

## Dressed for Success, Not Bucking Bales

Years later, I was driving home from an appointment. I was dressed in slacks, one of my nicest $55 shirts and a tie. It was one of those days when you could tell it was going to rain. I had my window down and the smell of cut alfalfa wafted through my car. It brought back great childhood memories. As I came over a hill, I noticed an old Allis-Chalmers tractor moving slowly down the field. An elderly man was driving a hay wagon with no kids putting up hay bales. I felt something was wrong with this picture. Indeed, there was nobody helping this old man. His hay was going to get wet and he was going to lose this cutting. I decided to approach him to see if he could use some help.

I knew he was thinking, "What is some city slicker doing pulling me over while I am trying to get my hay bales in?"

I asked if he could use a hand. He was chewing on a little weed and said, "It don't look like you'd be much use."

He didn't say another word, put the tractor in gear and started slowly down the field again. I secured my tie around my head as a sweatband and began bucking bales up on the wagon. I used to have a good skill where I would hurry to the farthest row and throw the last bale to the next row. Then I'd throw both of them to the next row. Then I'd lift all three on the wagon, jump up and stack them. Then I would repeat the process until the field was cleared.

I was going 90 to nothing and, to be honest, was pretty proud that I still had it! About the time I was finishing up it just started to rain. My shirt was a mess and my hands were scuffed up. I triumphantly sat down on a short stretch of fence when that old farmer pulled up and said, "Looks sure can be mighty deceiving."

Then he just took off. He never said, "Thank you," or anything else.

All my life I have been aware that you don't really know people until you get to know them. Your first impression might be correct but it might also be profoundly inaccurate.

## Solutions are Not Always Obvious

I love life and I have always had goals of what I want to do. They haven't always been well formed or planned out but they have always been there. At times, they have frustrated me because I want them to happen now. I figure if I came up with the idea, it must be a good one! You probably already know that life doesn't always work that way, but there were many times I just had to learn the hard way.

## Selling Seeds

As a 7-year-old boy I wanted a sleeping bag and a tent. I loved fishing and camping so I wanted to outfit myself right. I grew up in a small town in Pennsylvania, however, and we didn't have much money. So, if I was going to get my tent, I was going to have to figure out a way to earn the money. I asked my mom and she said I could try selling seeds. My mom bought a box of seeds and I figured I would be effective with some of the ladies in our area because they all loved to pinch my cheeks and comment on my big dimples.

Mom said, "Go sell these seeds," so I went next door and knocked on the door. When the lady of the house answered I said to her, "You don't want to buy any of these seeds do you?"

Of course, she didn't because of the way I went about my sales pitch. After being told, "No," I sat down by the ditch and pondered how I could do this better.

At the next house I opened up with, "Do you want to buy any of these seeds?" She looked at my box and said, "This side has lots of flowers and that side has vegetables. I will take flowers because they are pretty." She bought one pack of seeds. I was thrilled to have my first sale and I realized I had just learned something about my product.

I modified my presentation for the third house, "I have flowers and I have vegetables. Which one would you like?" She said, "I like flowers. My husband likes vegetables. We will take one of each."

That same pattern repeated itself for the next couple of houses. Once again, I stopped to think about what I was doing. I was glad to be selling seeds but I was walking too much and selling too little. I figured there was probably a better way to go about this venture.

At my next house I stepped it up.

"I am just a little boy selling good looking flowers and quality vegetables. I have come all the way to your house because I was pretty sure you would love them." I then set the box down and held up as many packs as my little hands could hold.

"These are for you," I would say to the wife holding out the flower seeds. "And these are for him," I would add holding the vegetable seeds out toward the husband.

Amazingly, they would buy everything I had in my hands. I had just learned something very important about the people in my community. I found a formula that would allow me to sell boxes of seeds not just packs of seeds. My motivation soared and I started going out every day that my mom would let me. I was usually late getting home because I kept going to houses with handfuls of seeds until they were all sold!

It wasn't long until I was able to get my sleeping bag and a tent.

## Apple Cider is Better than Smashed Apples

You think I would have figured out how it works from that experience but we are all stubborn! When I was 14-years-old, I wanted to buy some camera equipment. I was studying photography in school and discovered I was pretty good at it. I decided that I really needed a professional camera to reach my potential. It was expensive, however, and I didn't have the money to purchase it. I asked my dad and the farmer I was working for but neither of them was willing to advance me the money.

As only a 14-year-old can do, I got angry and took it out on the apple orchard. I plopped myself down among the trees and noticed a bunch of apples sitting on the ground. I began picking them up one by one and throwing them at the trees. Each splat of the apple helped me express my anger. Splat, splat, splat. At first, it felt good. I felt like I was showing my dad and that stingy farmer how right I was and how wrong they were. After about 20 minutes of throwing apples, however, it dawned on me that I was being silly.

The money I needed was sitting right in front of me and I was throwing it away.

Just like when I was selling seeds, I sat down and pondered what I could do differently. I gathered up a bunch of crates and went to find 5 of my friends. I bet them that I could fill crates faster than any of them could.

"If I can't fill these crates faster than you, I will pay you $15 to split between you," I announced, knowing they would do just about anything for $15.

The thought of beating me and making money was too much for them to resist so they took the challenge. They filled up crates frantically until I had an entire wagon full of apples. They "won" the bet so it only cost me $15 to get all the apples I needed to make apple cider. From that wagon of apples, I produced 30 gallons of cider which I was able to sell at the corner of the road for a $1 per gallon. When my friends figured out what I had done, they got mad at me. I appeased them, however, by agreeing to hire them to work other corners if they would help gather apples for free. We all made money and we all thought we were smart businessmen!

Often, we were not able to sell all the cider. I figured I would either have to throw it away or store it for the next year. I didn't realize that cider would get "hard" as you kept it in storage. In fact, I didn't even know what it meant for cider to become "hard." The men, however, understood completely so they took a keen interest in the "old" cider and began offering $2 per gallon.

When people in the community realized I was committed to doing this, they showed me how to make vinegar from the cider and another market opened up. For a few years, I was the go to guy for apple cider in our town. Again, it wasn't long until I was able to purchase the camera I wanted.

### Having a Plan is Always Better than Not Having a Plan

I got into the financial business because I noticed too many people are operating without a plan for their wealth. They believe their money is important. They work hard, or worked hard for years, to develop an income that could support them and their loved ones. They sincerely want to help the people they love. There was nothing wrong with their effort. There was nothing wrong with their desires. Many of them, however, agonized at the end of their lives because they didn't have a plan in place that gave them confidence their money would benefit the people they wanted to help.

I certainly understand why people find themselves living without a plan.

- Some people are young and full of dreams. They aren't aware yet of the need to have a structured plan. They believe they have time. They believe they will be strong for a long time. They believe they live in a world of opportunity. For most people, these statements are true since people do stay strong and remain productive for decades. For some, however, the dreams turn into nightmares in a moment. Sickness suddenly takes the life of a loved one. A disabling accident robs you of your ability to earn an income. An "act of nature" destroys your home exposing the fact that your insurance coverage is inadequate. A business mistake embroils you in a protracted law suit. You didn't expect that any of these experiences would be part of your journey so you didn't set up fences to protect vulnerable assets that didn't appear vulnerable.

- Some people suffer a divorce midway through life that disrupts their financial life. You certainly didn't plan on a divorce and would never have thought to organize your finances with this in mind. You had no idea how to predict the impact of splitting your estate and figuring out child support.

- Some people unexpectedly get laid off only to find it nearly impossible to find work. One year, two years, three years go by without employment ruining your confidence and developing a self-defeating mindset. Relinquishing your home back to the mortgage company only adds to the evidence of failure.

- Some people are simply disappointed with how their work environment turned out. You made plans based on assumptions of promotions you would receive. You set your budget based on raises in pay you counted on. You made financial commitments that would have been manageable if you had kept progressing in your career. But then, a younger person was given the position you had spent years working toward. Someone with more education but less experience was made your supervisor.

It became clear to me that working on finances without a plan is like building fences without including a gate. You can't get assets in the right field if you have no gate to access the pasture. You can't move assets around if you have no gate to help transition from one area to another. Fields become prisons if all they have are fences and no gate. The assets you want to put in don't get in. The assets you want to get out, can't get out. Your financial plan creates the gate that allows you to move resources around so the fences can protect the assets that matter to you.

## Life is Made Up of Seasons

The simplest way I know to strategically think about your financial plan is to compare it to farming crops. There is a time for planting, a time for growing and a time for harvesting. Each of these seasons has its unique goals, uses strategic tools and must be done in its time.

During the planting season you initialize your plan. A farmer tills the ground and plants seeds in anticipation of producing a high yield. The seeds appear to disappear in the ground but in reality they are preparing to become much larger! It is hard work and there is no glamor in the process. When the seeds are placed, it doesn't look like anything has been done. The crop is not accessible and it must be left undisturbed for a long time if it is going to work. In your financial plan, this is the time when you set up accounts and investment tools that will make assets inaccessible to you for long periods of time so they can produce a harvest later in life.

The growing season is a combination of maintenance and waiting. Weeds must be removed. Fertilizer must be applied. Unfruitful stalks must be pruned. Water must be monitored and added in as necessary. In one sense, the crops must be left alone so they can reach maturity. In another sense, they must be fed and protected so the growth doesn't get disrupted by bugs, disease, drought or overgrowth. In your financial plan, this is the time you consistently add to your accounts, do regular reviews of the tools you are using to grow your investments and seek out proper coverages to safeguard the growth in your assets.

The harvesting season is the time when you reap what you have sown. The crops are full grown and ready to be collected and utilized. If the farmer begins too soon the crops won't be ripe and the effort will be wasted. If the crops are left "on the vine" too long they spoil and fall off, or, varmints will sneak in overnight and "steal" the crop. Every farmer knows that timing is vital in transferring their crops from the plant to the market. It was the main focus of the whole process from the first day the ground was plowed.

Our finances have a harvest time just as crops do but it seems harder for people to admit this. The thought of taking our investments out of a financial tool that is focused on growth and placing them in a "different" vehicle that seems more like storage is a hard transition. We want to keep believing that the growth will continue and that we may just hit a windfall year that expands our resources beyond our projections. If you have plenty of money and can afford to lose some of it, keeping it in riskier investments may make sense for you. Most of us, however, fare better if we "harvest" our investments later in life and place our funds in investments that are specifically designed for harvest.

**Transplanting Tomatoes**

It may be overwhelming to some of you to think of a field of crops so let me give a much simpler example involving tomatoes grown at your house. When you first plant the tomato plant, you place a seed in a small container and water it regularly. You rejoice when the first sprout appears and continue to feed and water it on schedule. It doesn't take long until the plant is too big for the small container you began with. You instinctively know that the plant must be transplanted to a larger container. If you don't dig up the plant and put it in a bigger space, the plant will either stop growing or die altogether. You don't move the plant because you are trying to harm it. You move it because you are trying to facilitate its growth potential. The plant has moved from the planting phase to the growth phase. As the plant continues to grow, blossoms will appear. The flowers soon transform into small, green tomatoes. As you continue to nurture the plant, the tomatoes grow in size and turn bright red. At some point, you will reach the conclusion that the fruit has reached its full size. The tomatoes are "ripe" and will need to be picked in order to get the value they can bring to your life. If you don't harvest them and put them to a different use they will dwindle and lose their value.

With tomatoes, moving from one stage to another tends to be instinctive. By looking at the plant, you know when it is time to transplant to a larger growth environment. By checking the tomatoes periodically, it also becomes obvious when it is time to pick the crop and put them to use. All of us, however, are much more emotional about our money than we are about tomatoes. As a result, it can be difficult to recognize when our money needs to be transplanted and when it needs to be harvested. This is where a well-crafted financial plan can help you map out your decisions.

## Humility Trumps Pride and Ego

When it comes to financial planning, one of the most effective tools you can apply is humility. Humility is nothing more than taking an honest look at life and making decisions based upon the way life really is. Let me give you an example.

You have probably heard about the stock market and mutual funds. Mutual funds are a collection of stocks put together by a portfolio manager in an effort to create a consistent yield. There are also more aggressive stock strategies that have the potential for larger returns in exchange for the risk of potentially large losses. When you are young, active in your career and have decades of earning potential ahead of you, the stock market offers a viable and attractive option for your investments. Even if a risky investment went south, you would realistically have time to recover from the losses. In this case, humility says you will take calculated risks. If you are afraid of risk, you will seek out people who can help you asses what is appropriate so your natural instincts don't keep you from opportunities that would benefit you. If you tend to be reckless, humility will lead you to advisers who can help you assess the wisdom of the big leaps you are instinctively willing to take.

When you are seventy years old, it is a different story. For most people who are 70 or over, their financially productive years are behind them. Risky investments no longer make as much sense as they did 30 years before. A large loss at this time of life could prove to be devastating, not just for a season but for the rest of your life. Not because you are less talented than you used to be but because you simply have less time. In this case, humility will lead you to safer, more predictable investments. You will hear plenty of reports about investments that could make you more money than tools that guarantee a steady return. It is easy for your ego to drive the ship with the idea that you want to get in on the action. To be sure, there are some great investments out there. It is always possible that an investment decision you make will succeed greatly but it is just as likely you will lose money on the deal. If you are not careful, pride can blind you to the risks as you overinflate the opportunities. Some risks that are good during our highly productive years are just not wise during the silver season of life.

## Keep Dancing

Getting out of the Navy was a significant transition in my life. I enjoyed being a Navy Corpsman but I knew I didn't want a career in the medical field. I loved photography but the advances in technology turned everybody into a self-proclaimed photographer and I figured that would be a hard way to make a living. One day I saw an ad in the paper for part-time ballroom dance instructors. I had always been good at athletics and had natural rhythm so I thought I would give it a shot. I went to dance training and attended their sales instruction and caught on to both quickly. After just one week, I was selling competitions and enrolling in competitions myself. It was another reminder that we all ought to look for areas of natural ability to invest our time and talent.

Shortly after I started giving dance lessons, Marge walked in the studio wearing a big diamond ring.

She confided in me, "My husband and I used to dance before he passed away." I could tell by the look in her eyes that it was a very precious part of her life.

"Would he like it if you still danced?" I asked. When Marge nodded her head I said, "Let's dance like you two used to."

She was thrilled by the idea so I ran her credit card for six months of dance lessons and a competition. Nobody told me that I couldn't sell her that many lessons and she didn't hesitate. I found out later the standard protocol was to sell an introductory plan that included two or three private sessions and a group lesson. She wasn't looking for a few lessons, however, she was looking to dance! She was willing to invest the money because she wanted to compete in social dance to feel young and alive again. She didn't care if she ever won but she was intent on dancing just like her and her husband used to do.

Just like Marge, you have a skill, an interest or an activity that makes you feel alive and whole. For her, it was dancing. For you, it may be something different. Hopefully you will be able to do the things that help you enjoy life as long as possible. Marge had planned her money so she was able to keep dancing. As you humbly and diligently put your plan to work, you can set up your life so you can keep dancing too!

# Chapter 2

# BUILDING FENCES

I grew up in a rural town in Pennsylvania. We raised crops, goats, bees, chickens and a collection of rabbits. My dad was proud of his property and he worked hard to keep it productive. In addition, I worked for a number of the dairy farmers in our community who were glad to have the help. I also worked as a farm hand for many of our Amish neighbors doing everything from fixing fences to threshing wheat. For both my dad and the farmers, I had the "privilege" of working hard.

One of the keys to making the farms work were the fences. My dad built fences to keep the animals in the areas he wanted them to be and keep predators out. In order for the fences to be effective they needed to be intact and there had to be a functioning gate so that animals could be moved when necessary.

As a kid, you would have thought I actually owned the animals because I heard the same phrase over and over . . .

"Mark, your cows are out, you need to go round them up."

"Mark, your chickens are out, go chase them down and get them back in the pen."

"Mark, your rabbits are out, we'll see you later after you gather them up."

My mom was a real sport when it came to rounding up animals. There were many mornings when she would come outside in her housecoat to help me catch the wandering critters even as the school bus was pulling up.

My cows, my chickens, my rabbits. I looked forward with

anticipation to the day we took "my animals" to the market to sell them for a profit. I dreamed of the things I would buy. I knew, of course, they weren't mine but it was fun to dream about making money from "my livestock," even if just for a few minutes. As soon as I arrived at the auction, they magically transformed back into my dad's animals or the farmer's livestock!

I learned an important lesson, despite my disappointment. The responsibility that leads to wealth is every bit as important as the wealth itself. The livestock was a vital source of income for our family while I was growing up. The animals didn't just sell themselves, however. In order to see a profit, the following tasks needed to be done on a regular basis:

- The gate needed to be closed every time.
- Sometimes the gate needed to be checked because the animals would figure out how to get It open.
- The fence line needed to be inspected on a regular basis.
- Fences needed to be repaired any time they were damaged. There were multiple ways the fences could be damaged. Trees could fall on them. Weather could blow them apart. Animals could put stress on them. Weeds could overtake them. I noticed that the fence never repaired itself!
- If we ever expanded our operation, new fences needed to be built.

I didn't realize it at the time but I was forming my understanding of how a solid financial plan works. In order to develop a healthy plan for your finances that will provide throughout your life, there are several principles that must be in play.

### Assets are Valuable

My goats, chickens and rabbits were valuable to me. They provided food for our family and funds for our bank account. The healthier they were, the healthier we were. I wanted my animals to be well fed, happy and in good physical condition. I didn't build fences to build fences. I built them to protect the valuable assets in my life. I inspected and repaired them to protect those same assets. And, I closed the gate because I didn't want to lose the assets.

In the same way, you have an income, savings and investments that are valuable to you. You have worked hard to acquire them. You have sacrificed to both accumulate them and increase their value. Nobody dreams of retiring with nothing and having to depend on loved ones to provide for them. We all dream of producing an income during our lives that will take care of our families and then take care of us. So, before we go any farther, let me congratulate you on acquiring the assets you currently own.

In fact, can you take a moment right now and say, "These are my assets. I worked hard to acquire them. I want to do everything I can to protect them because they are valuable and they belong to me and my loved ones."

## Assets Need to be Fenced In

I have always found it amusing that animals like to wander. Every cow, goat, chicken and rabbit I ever worked with would wander away given the opportunity. It wasn't as if they were sitting around plotting ways to escape. Can you picture that conversation?

Cow 1: "Hey buddy. Do you want to escape?'

Cow 2: "What does escape mean?"

Cow 1: "You know, get out."

Cow 2: "Get out of where?"

Cow 1: "Get out of here?"

Cow 2: "Why would we want to do that?"

Cow 1: "Because."

Cow 2: "Okay. Yeah, I want to get out. What will we do when we get out?"

Cow 1: "That's a dumb question. We just need to get out."

Cow 2: "Your right, let's go."

No, they don't plot their escape. They are just prone to wander. In the same way, money is prone to wander. If you don't fence it in, it will get spent or squandered to the point that you wake up one day and it is gone. You didn't mean to deplete the resource, the fence was just down and the assets headed out.

## Fences can be Fun

Putting up fences is hard work but sometimes it can be fun. When kids from the city would visit our farm, I would look for a reason to show them our pasture. As we got close to the electric fence, I would make up some reason for us to hold hands. Then I would grab hold of the fence. Since they were at the end of the chain, the charge from the fence would hit them accompanied by squealing and hopping around.

My brother was dating the lady who is now his wife. They were taking a leisurely walk along the fence line. I am sure they were having a great time talking calmly and probably laughing. For some reason, my brother thought it would be funny to introduce his attractive girlfriend to the joys of the electric fence. They stopped by the fence and looked affectionately at each other. He leaned in a little to see if there was any interest on her part. She leaned in a little closer as their lips moved toward one another. In a moment of romantic bliss their lips touched in a heartwarming and thrilling moment. Just then, my brother reached back and grabbed onto the fence. I am sure it was the first electrically charged kiss she had ever experienced! The shocked look on her face was priceless. My brother told me later he saw her express sweet affection, surprise, anger and laughter all in one kiss. Afterward, she told the story to everyone with an "I can't believe he did that" tone. It must have worked, however, because they are still married today.

The Gate needs to be Checked Regularly

Growing up, one of my favorite times of the day was lunch. The following scene happened many times:

"Mark, lunch is ready," my mom, or the lady of the house if I was working for a farmer, would shout from the front porch.

I would come running from the field because I knew mom had a spread of delicious food ready for consumption. I would sit down and stare at the food dreaming about what I would eat first. Everyone else would find their way to the table and share the news of the morning. We weren't allowed to eat until everyone was seated and dad, or one of the other farmers, had prayed over the meal. The conversation would wane in anticipation of the sacred moment when dad would pray.

Invariably, dad or the farmer would ask before he prayed, "Mark, did you check the fence and the gates before you came in?"

You have heard the old saying about strategic situations, "You should never ask a question for which you don't know the answer." Well, the men already knew that I had not checked the gates as they dismissed me from the table.

Of course, the animals were out because the gate was left open or they had found a hole in the fence. I would spend the next hour chasing the herd back into the pasture trying to get it done as quickly as possible so I could get back to lunch. When I finally got back in the house, the "feast" I had dreamed about was nothing more than slim pickings—a faint reminder of what might have been.

I didn't mean to overlook the gate and it didn't seem necessary to check all the fences. I certainly didn't want to miss out on lunch. Besides, the fences were fine yesterday so it was easy to assume they were in good shape today. I was just too excited about other things. I knew the gate was closed earlier in the morning so checking it seemed boring and mundane. Our finances are the same way. None of us intend to lose money. None of us want to miss out on a well planned retirement income. None of us want to run out of money before we run out of years. Therefore, we need to have a plan for checking the gate and monitoring our fences to make sure our money is where we want it to be when we want it to be there.

## What are the Fences Protecting?

The reason we have fences is there is something we want to protect. We want to keep valuable assets inside and dangerous forces out. In our personal lives, what are we trying to protect with our financial fences?

*Physical Health.* First and foremost is your health. If you are physically healthy and confident your medical needs are being addressed, you will have energy for work, stamina for your pursuits and enthusiasm in your important relationships. It is, therefore, in your best interests to take care of your body and have health professionals involved in your life.

On a more cautious note, healthcare costs have a greater potential to drain your financial resources than anything else in your life. I certainly hope you never get devastating news from your doctor that changes the trajectory of your life but I can't promise it won't happen.

My consistent reminder is Barry. He proudly attended his daughter's high school graduation. Kim had good grades, good friends and a good future ahead of her. Barry and Carol looked lovingly in each other's eyes relishing the moment in their daughter's life.

They all assumed the trip to the doctor that summer would be a minor inconvenience in an otherwise stellar year. The word "cancer" changed all of that. The words "inoperable," "fast moving" and "aggressive" were almost too much to process.

After the funeral I had the chance to sit down with Barry.

"How are you doing with all this?" I asked.

"I am doing better than I thought I would. The past few months have been pretty incredible. As hard as it is to watch one of your kids pass, I learned more from my daughter about how to live than anyone else I have ever met. What made it possible was our insurance coverage. Our agent 'talked us into' getting coverage we weren't sure we even needed but boy am I glad now. He had the insight to recommend coverage we would have never considered on our own. It was spot on, however. We were able to spend the time with Kim rather than having to raise money in our community. Otherwise, I would have felt like we were robbed of the time we were supposed to have with our daughter. Knowing the needs were met helped us all relax and focus on what really mattered. I will forever be grateful to him"

This is just one example of why health coverage and supplemental insurance is so vital. You want to have confidence that your regular medical needs can be addressed and you want to have protection in place if the unexpected or unfortunate happens. Health insurance guarantees your doctor will be paid but what about you? Supplemental coverage is your promise to yourself that you will be paid also if you lose the ability to work for a period of time. Without these safeguards, an otherwise smooth journey in life can be turned into a frightening rollercoaster ride.

*Your Home.* For most people, the largest investment of your life will be your home. You will carry a mortgage for decades. You will build some of your most precious memories in the place you live. You will interact with the most important people in your life there. It will be a place of comfort and connection.

That is why losing a home is emotionally devastating to most people. We all understand the structure is just building materials that have no intrinsic value in themselves. But, the space they form becomes the stage on which our lives are lived out. The extent to which you can protect this major investment will help provide a sense of peace and stability to you and your loved ones.

*Bank Accounts.* As you produce an income, you will choose to place the money somewhere. For most people this means having one or several bank accounts. This is your money and you trust your bank to take care of it for you until such time as you need it.

Investments. In addition to bank accounts you may have investments that include real estate, stocks, bonds or precious metals.

*Retirement Accounts.* These are funds you set up to access later in life. The hope is they accumulate money and grow over the years to provide a consistent income when you retire.

## What Fences Should I Build?

Just to remind all of us, we don't want to build fences just to build fences. We build fences to protect valuable assets. In the world of your personal finances, you may find the following fences useful:

- Life Insurance. Most people I have ever met have a desire to leave money to their loved ones. One of the most common and effective ways to accomplish this is through life insurance.
- Health Insurance. It is nearly impossible to picture a scenario in which some type of healthcare coverage is not necessary. You may have coverage provided by your employer, Medicare coverage or an individual policy that addresses your needs. In any case, part of your financial plan should include discussions with your adviser on the adequacy of your coverage. In certain cases, you may also want to consider carrying supplemental insurance to address possibilities such as cancer or disability.
- Property and Casualty Insurance. Your home is an important place in your life. Hopefully you will never experience a

calamity with your house. It is great to consider that you may get all the way through life with only maintenance concerns with your house. You know, however, that you can't predict whether or not this will be your story. Weather, other people's careless (or malicious) actions or other acts of nature need to be accounted for. This is why being acquainted with a public adjustor and carrying a policy that can cover the value of your home is part of your fence. Feel free to contact me if you need information on either of these important resources for protecting your home and property.

- Revocable Living Trust. Today you have the opportunity to make decisions about your home, your bank accounts, your possessions and your investments. A day is coming, however, when those decisions will be made by someone else. With a revocable living trust, you have the opportunity to determine how these decisions will be made and who will benefit from the assets you have accumulated throughout your life. In the absence of a living trust, your estate may have to go through probate which will take control away from your loved ones and place it in the hands of the courts. The chapter on trusts will give you more information but feel free to contact me if you need a referral for trusted legal assistance on this.

- Annuities. Annuities, like life insurance policies, are offered by insurance companies and are backed by the financial strength of the company itself. An annuity is an agreement you make to give some amount of money to the company in exchange for a guaranteed income at a later date. The most common annuities are pension plans offered by employers but there are many other varieties that can meet your particular needs. This fence keeps today's assets in your possession to provide for future needs.

- Long Term Care. Hopefully, you are going to

live a long life filled with unforgettable memories with your family members and friends. If you get this privilege, at some point personal care and health related care are going to become quite expensive. If you are not prepared, these extreme needs can quickly deplete your personal resources. If you have a plan for long term care, however, these years can be indelible for you and your loved ones as you peacefully reminisce about the legacy of your family.

## Hunters and Fishermen

As I was growing up I noticed fences would often get damaged by hunters and fishermen. The pastures were often near great hunting land so hunters would climb our fences in an attempt to get to their prey. They would scale one fence, cross the pasture, then scale the fence on the other side as they chased their prized game. Often the climbing would loosen elements of the fence creating openings for "my" animals to escape. I noticed that hunters never came back to fix the fences they loosened up. They might apologize at times but it was always up to me and the farmer to fix the openings in the fence.

At other times, fishermen would hike across the property to get to a fishing hole. Crossing the pasture would provide a shortcut so they could spend more time fishing. It never bothered the farmers but, like the hunters, their journey would often loosen the gates providing openings in an otherwise solid enclosure.

Again, I didn't realize as a kid that I was looking at a picture of possible dangers to people's financial lives. In the financial world, hunters are the people who would like to have what you possess. They can be unscrupulous thieves or they can be greedy professionals but they have the same goal. They want to transfer what you own into their hands. Fishermen are trying to see what you own through public records. This is why so many wills are contested in court. Some estimates even report that 1 in 3 wills are successfully overturned in probate court.

## Include the Gate

Can you imagine a beautiful pasture surrounded by a well-built fence that has no gate? We would all talk about it as a profound joke. We would be tempted to say things such as:

"That is a beautiful place but where is the gate?"

"What was that guy thinking? He spent all that time and money on a fence but forgot to install a gate?"

"Sure nothing will get out of that pasture but nothing will get in either!"

"That guy must get tired jumping the fence every time he wants to get in his pasture."

"Wow, whoever built that fence is going to be out of business soon. I don't want them building my fence!"

The gate that keeps your assets in, prevents damaging factors from getting in and provides access to your estate is your financial plan. In my experience, most people have a casual financial plan. What I mean by that is their plan is not written down anywhere and it is never evaluated by anyone who works in the field. You have dreams in your heart and you have chosen certain steps to fund that dream but you never coordinated your decisions in a decisive, delineated plan.

Your estate plan does not have to be complicated or hard to understand. It is simply your desire and decisions written down in a cohesive scheme to help you reach your goals. Your financial plan will provide your personal answers to the following questions:

- What season of my financial journey am I currently facing?
- How much cash do we have on hand?
- What are our primary ways of producing income?
- How much of our income do we want to save?
- How much income do you want during

retirement?
- What combination of tools will provide this income?
- How much assistance will my spouse need if I lose my ability to produce an income?
- How much do you want to leave for your heirs?
- What combination of tools will provide this inheritance?
- How much insurance do you need on your home?
- What type of health coverage do you need?
- How will you provide for your long term care needs?

You may be able to figure out some of this on your own but most likely you will need to meet with a financial adviser who can help you evaluate your particular needs and desires. A compassionate and competent adviser will also be able to expose you to tools that will help you reach your goals.

**Mike the Mechanic**
Whenever I think of the value of a trusted financial adviser, I think of Mike my mechanic. I drive a lot so I have an ongoing relationship with my truck. I can tell when it is running well and I can tell when it needs attention. I can easily keep track of regular maintenance but when the truck makes a strange noise or runs different than I am used to, I take it to Mike. I know it needs attention but that doesn't mean that I know what it needs in detail. Mike has experience. Mike has studied diligently. Mike has skill in this arena of life. As a result, I like to ask Mike three questions, "Can you please fix this? How much will it cost? When can I get my truck back?"

Sometimes I feel ignorant when I talk to Mike. "Hi Mike. Can you look at my truck? It is making a strange sound."

"What kind of noise is it making?"

"It is kind of like a growling."

"A growling? What do you mean?"

"You know, Mike, it sounds like it is growling at me?"

"I am not sure I do know, Mark. Can you make the sound for me?"

"You know, like ggggrrrrrrow." I wanted to get it right so I leaned into it, contorted my face and tried my best to push the sound up from my diaphragm.

Mike couldn't control himself and started laughing at me. He said, "Sorry, Mark, I couldn't help myself. I think the U-joint that comes off your transfer case connecting the driveshaft to the rear differential is wearing out. Mike reeled off his description like everyone knows what these words mean. Some of you, to be sure, know exactly what he was talking about. For others, he may as well have been talking Russian or Arabic to someone who only knows English.

In the same way people often feel inadequate when it comes to talking about financial planning. The adviser who spends every week interacting with financial goals and products will talk with ease about margins, interest rates, indexing, riders, policies and other financial terms. At times, it all makes sense to you but at times it seems like a foreign language. The key is to find an adviser who will take the time to identify your goals, understand what you need to know and fill in the gaps from his expertise.

When this gate is in place, you will know what to invest, when to invest it, how to protect your assets and how to mobilize your money when it is time to fund your retirement.

## Section 1

---

# INCOME PLANNING

# Chapter 3

# LAUGH AT THE FUTURE

W e all have to engage in retirement planning even though we would, if possible, just as soon ignore it because we don't like the implications. We all want to feel young forever and would love to think that funding our future will magically happen simply because we are good people. That makes for a good script in a sentimental movie but is just wishful thinking in real life. In the real world, it is in our best interest to make plans for the day we have less stamina, focus and energy than we possess today.

**Laugh at the Future**

Preparing for retirement begins with shaping your attitude. Growing old enough to retire is one of life's great achievements and ought to be celebrated. Cultivating a good sense of humor as you age is one of the most effective ways to instill a positive attitude in yourself and those around you. According to helpguide. org, laughter will positively affect you in the following ways:

*Laughter relaxes the whole body.* A good, hearty laugh relieves physical tension and stress, leaving your muscles relaxed for up to 45 minutes after.

*Laughter boosts the immune system.* Laughter decreases stress hormones while it increases immune cells and infection-fighting antibodies, thus improving your resistance to disease.

*Laughter triggers the release of endorphins*, the body's natural feel-good chemicals. Endorphins promote an overall sense of well-being and can even temporarily relieve pain.

*Laughter protects the heart.* Laughter improves the function of blood vessels and increases blood flow, which can help protect you against a heart attack and other cardiovascular problems.[1]

When you think about your future, start with a good laugh:

## Pholenfrometry

A medical transcriber related the following experience:

We were really confused. While transcribing medical audiotapes, a colleague came upon the following garbled diagnosis: "This man has pholenfrometry." Knowing nothing about that particular condition, she double-checked with the doctor. After listening to the tape, he shook his head.

"This man," he said, translating for her, "has fallen from a tree."[2]

## Preparing Your Plan

Whether you realize it or not, you already have a plan in place. It may be a well-defined, regularly funded, consistently evaluated plan that has you feeling pretty good about your future. Or, it may be a blindly hopeful plan like Bob:

**Bob:** Do you have a retirement plan?

**Ted:** Yup, lottery tickets.

**Bob:** Lottery tickets? That's it?

**Ted:** Of course not. Retirement Plan B is to sue some mega-corporation for a million bucks.[3]

More likely, your plan is somewhere between well-defined and blindly hopeful. You have taken some steps toward creating an income for your future because you agree with Zig Ziglar who said, "Money isn't the most important thing in life, but it's reasonably close to oxygen on the 'gotta have it' scale."[4] Your plan has more likely been in reaction to what others have sincerely told you rather than a deliberate plan based on wise insight. You found people you could trust and followed their advice.

Good advice is a great place to start but at some point it has to become your plan based on your conclusions about what is right for your financial future. Putting together a plan for retirement income is a lot like building a puzzle. There are pieces that must fit together to create a whole picture. The crazy thing about this puzzle, however, is that you get to design your own box top that gives shape to your income. Don't let this intimidate you. You can't predict everything you will face in the future but you can put together a plan that makes sense and see how it turns out. The world is filled with stories of successful people who made plans only to see those plans turn into something different than they expected.

## Murphy's Law

Captain Edward A. Murphy, Jr. was an engineer with the US Air Force. In 1949 he created the harness for a rocket-powered sled designed to move faster than a speeding bullet. The goal was to test how much acceleration and deceleration a human being could tolerate. The test failed and the sled's passenger (Major John Paul Stapp) was temporarily blinded because - as Murphy later discovered - every one of the harness' gauges had been installed backward.

Exasperated, Murphy made a snide comment that if there were two ways to do something and one could result in catastrophe, someone would invariably choose to do it the catastrophic way. His colleagues overheard him and began repeating the adage. Before long, "Murphy's Law" caught on and became widely quoted. It was even added to Webster's Dictionary in 1958.[5]

## Keep Working the Plan

As you plan for your retirement, don't be too hard on yourself. Some of your choices will be brilliant and very effective. Others will surprise you with an unexpected outcome. Together, they form a plan that will provide for you and your loved ones if you keep working your plan and choose to laugh at the future!

*Chapter 4*

# IDENTIFY YOUR INCOME

The process of determining your retirement income is exactly that – a process. Like following a recipe to make a great meal or responding to a GPS to complete a trip, planning for your future is made up of deliberate steps that build on one another. In time, what started as hopeful projections will develop into an action plan that actually generates income.

The driving questions for this process are obvious to most people. In fact, I would venture to predict you have asked these questions yourself because they are so basic to our natural fears and motivations in life. The questions are:

- *Will I have enough money to live on when I retire?*
- *How long will my money last?*
- If I live to be 60, 70, 80 or beyond, will I still be able to support myself?

Dave Erhard points out the scenario none of us wants to face when we enter our data into one of the many retirement calculators available on the internet:

"According to your latest data, if you retire today, you can live reasonably well until 5 p.m. tomorrow."[6]

## Identify Sources of income during retirement

Let's look at steps you can start taking starting today that will help you prepare for retirement with an income that works for you.

### Social Security

Most of us will be able to take advantage of the Social Security system. Social Security became part of the American landscape when President Franklin D. Roosevelt signed into law the Social Security Act on August 14, 1935. The act was part of a comprehensive program to combat the effects of the great Depression during the early 1930s. Millions of Americans either had no job or couldn't earn enough money to feed their families. The nation was frustrated and frantic to find a solution. Social Security was originally developed to address the problem of unemployment. It quickly became a way of funding retirement since so many of the unemployed were elderly. In essence, the system created a process for workers to place a small percentage of their salary into an aggregate account. Later, when they retired, they would draw money out of the account to help with monthly expenses. It was never intended to be the sole source of retirement income but simply a safety net to make sure people were not impoverished. When the program was set up President Roosevelt emphatically stated, "we can never insure one hundred percent of the population against one hundred percent of the hazards and vicissitudes of life,"[7] but he did hope it would help avert many of the desperate situations people encountered during the depression.

Since that time, Social Security has become a standard deduction from your paycheck and a stable part of your retirement funding.

*Eligibility*: You become eligible for Social Security benefits when you have earned 40 credits which is equal to about 10 years of work. How do you accumulate credits?

Prior to 1978, whenever you worked for three months, you would earn one credit. That meant you could accumulate 4 credits per year as long as you had a job.

In 1978, the math changed a little. You could still earn 4 credits per year but it was based on how much you earned during the year rather than just the fact that you had a job. The amount you need to earn to qualify is not that high, however.

Since 2012, one credit is assigned to your Social Security account for every $1,130 you earn in wages (up to 4 per year).

In other words, all you need to do is work at a reasonable pace and you will qualify for this portion of your retirement income.

*Receiving Benefits:* The idea behind Social Security is to provide some level of benefit to you until the end of your life. It certainly won't allow you to retire in luxury but it was never intended for that. It will simply keep you out of poverty. It is up to you when you want to begin receiving your Social Security income. You can begin anytime between 62 and 70. By the time you reach 70, you must begin to receive payments but you can begin sooner than that if you choose. If you elect to receive benefits before age 70, you want to keep in mind that the amount you will receive each month will be lower.

The Social Security Agency has an amount in mind they will pay you over the length of your retirement. Using actuarial tables, they have estimated how long they believe you will live and have based your benefits on that estimate. For example, let's say they expect you to live until you are 85 years old. If you begin taking payments at 70, they will divide the amount they have assigned to you over a 15 year period. If you choose to begin receiving payments at 63, they will divide that same amount over a 22 year period. You will get the same amount of money either way. You will just get less per month if you begin sooner. Keep in mind, the government will not stop paying you if you live longer than their estimate. The amount they commit to you is guaranteed for as long as you live so you can budget it into your future planning with confidence.

*Figuring Out Taxes.* When you receive Social Security benefits, they are technically subject to being taxed. Some of the income you receive, however, will be exempted because the program was set up to help people avoid poverty. It would not make sense for the government to set up a program to provide a minimum threshold for people then take a bunch of it back through taxes!

If, however, you have planned well and poverty is not an issue, the government will ask you to pay taxes. This may not sound like good news but your ability to pay taxes means you have planned well and you have sufficient income to enjoy your retirement years. The way the government figures out your taxable income once you begin receiving Social Security benefits is as follows:

*The Zero Percent Club:* If you are single and your income is less than $25,000 per year, none of your income will be taxed. If you are married and your combined income is $32,000 or less, you likewise will not be taxed. Your income will include all sources not just Social Security so don't base these calculations simply on the amount of your Social Security check.

*The Fifty Percent Club:* If your income is between $25,000 and $34,000 as a single person or between $32,000 and $44,000 as a married couple, 50% of the amount you receive from Social Security will be included in your taxable income.

*The Eighty-Five Percent Club:* 85% of your Social Security income will be taxable if your total income is more than $34,000 as an individual or more than $44,000 as a married couple.

I am sure this is more complicated than you would make it but that is just the way taxes are. When it comes to getting it right with our taxes many of us feel like the retired man who reported:

"I was at the Senior Center today and failed a Health and Safety course that was put on for us old fogies. One of the questions was: 'In the event of a fire, what steps would you take?'

"\*\*\*\*\*\*\* big ones was apparently the wrong answer . . ."[8]

This is why most people have an accountant or other tax professional help them when it is time to report to the IRS.

### Pension Plan

Some of you may be the beneficiary of a pension plan. If you work for a large company or if you have a union that represents workers in your field, your compensation package probably includes a pension agreement. In short, a pension is a contractual agreement between you and your employer that provides retirement income to you when you are done working for the company. A pension is different than personal retirement accounts in that your income is guaranteed. The pension plan is set up to pay a lifetime benefit, whereas a personal retirement fund will provide as long as there is money in the fund to make payouts.

There are a couple of ways that a pension can be calculated and, regardless of how the numbers are determined, the terms are laid out ahead of time so both you and your employer know what to expect. Examples of how pensions are calculated include:

*The Defined Benefit Plan.* In this scenario, your employer commits to pay you a specific amount of money for the rest of your life when you retire. Your lifelong benefit is based on a formula chosen by your employer that will take into account how long you work for the company, your salary and what age you choose to retire. The amount is outlined ahead of time and committed to on paper. The employer carries all the responsibility for choosing the investments that will fund your retirement and making contributions to the investment so there is enough money to make the payments they have agreed to.

*The Dollars Times Service Plan.* This plan is popular among unions and is based on the time you worked in your field. The employer will agree that a certain amount of income will be paid during retirement for every year of employment. For example, the plan may offer to pay you $100 per month during your retirement years for every year you were in the service of the employer. If you worked for 35 years, your monthly retirement income would be $3,500.

If you are married, you probably also have the option of choosing the "joint and survivor" option. This means that your spouse will be included in the annuity that funds your retirement. If your spouse happens to live longer than you, your retirement benefits will transfer to your surviving partner. Depending on how the pension is written, your surviving spouse may receive all or part of your regular monthly payments.

### 401k/ 403b

You have probably heard the term 401 (k). It didn't take too much creativity to assign this name because it comes from sub-section 401 (k) of the Internal Revenue Code. If you are working for a non-profit organization, such as a church employee or teacher, you may have heard of the 403(b), which is the non-profit equivalent of the 401(k). You will hear these plans referred to as defined-contribution pension accounts but don't let the long name confuse you. In simple terms, these are retirement accounts you put money into and you own. These plans create a pension fund that you, as the employee, make contributions to through your employer. You decide how much you want to have deducted from your paycheck and automatically deposited in a personal retirement savings account. This is designed to produce a retirement fund in your name over which you have more control. You have some decision-making authority over how much money gets contributed and how those funds will be invested each year. In some cases, your employer may even match funds so your account grows quicker.

The money that gets deducted from your paycheck and put in your 401(k) may or may not be tax-deferred, depending on what your specific plan allows. If the funds are tax-deferred, that means this amount will not be used to calculate your income tax while you are working. Whether the deductions from your paycheck are tax-deferred or not, any money your account earns through your investments will only be taxed when you begin to withdraw it during your retirement. This is good news and may lead you to ask, "Can I put my whole paycheck into my 401(k) and just live off my spouse's income?" The answer, of course, is no. You are limited to $17,500 per year that you can put in your 401(k).

The purpose of creating retirement pension accounts is to save money for the future. The longer you contribute and the more you invest, the more you will be able to "pay yourself" during retirement. Taking the money out early defeats the purpose and interrupts the earning potential of your investment. As a result, the Internal Revenue Code (IRS regulations) imposes a severe penalty if you withdraw money from your account early. The money is yours, so you have the freedom to access the funds when you want. Just keep in mind that it will cost you a significant amount in penalties to access it before the age of 59 ½.

### IRAs/Roth IRAs

In addition to pensions and 401(k) plans, every working individual in America has the opportunity to contribute to an Individual Retirement Account or IRA. IRAs come in two flavors. The traditional IRA and the Roth IRA.

The traditional IRA is an account, set up by an individual, for the express purpose of saving money for retirement. The contributions you make to your IRA are tax-deductible so you don't pay income tax on them until you begin to use the money in the future. It is a self-directed fund so you make the decisions about how the money is invested. You can choose an aggressive approach with the hope of significantly increasing your funds or you can take a more conservative approach with a focus on security.

Roth IRAs are likewise an account set up by an individual to save for the future. The difference is that funds you put in a Roth IRA are not tax-deductible. They will be included in the income you report to the IRS. With this being true, why would someone choose a Roth IRA? Well, there is a potential tax benefit later on. Since the money you invest in this type of investment has already been taxed, you can withdraw it "tax-free" later on. Also, there are fewer restrictions on how you can invest this money so you can take a riskier approach in your Roth IRA in hopes of a bigger return.

Whether you choose a traditional, Roth or combination of the two, the most you can contribute to your IRA per year is $5,500 (as of 2014). Since this is all based on IRS provisions, there are of course exceptions and conditions. You must be able to show taxable income on your tax return in order to put money into your IRA. If you are over 50 years old, you can also deposit an additional $1,000 per year for a total of $6,500. If you are married, your spouse can have his/her own IRA, even if you are the only one who earned taxable income during the year.

### Personal earnings

In addition to tax-deferred retirement accounts, you have the option of saving any amount of money you choose in a variety of investment options. You can have savings accounts, certificates of deposit, individual stocks or mutual funds, life insurance, annuities, and the list goes on. The money you invest in these options will be funded by your taxable income and the interest you earn will be added to your yearly income. That should never stop you, however, from investing if you have the money to do so. Make an appointment with your financial advisor to discuss your options so you can maximize your future income.

## What are Others Doing?

Some folks at Boston College decided it would be a good idea to figure out how people in America are funding their retirements. To guide their efforts, they created the Center for Retirement Research. To help communicate their findings more effectively, they divided retirees into three categories based on income levels: Bottom Income Tier, Middle Income Tier and Top Income Tier. For each of these tiers, they explored how much of each person's income came from the different sources of retirement funds. The most surprising result was the extent to which American retirees 65 and older rely on Social Security for their retirement income, even those who are at the top-third of the income bracket. The researchers displayed their findings in the pie charts below:

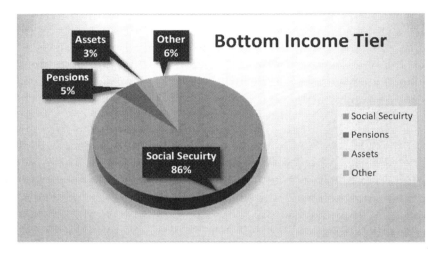

The Bottom Income Tier: This represents the 33% of Americans who are age 65 and above with an annual income of $16,758 or less in 2009. They receive their retirement income in the following average proportions:

86 percent from Social Security

5 percent from pensions (Traditional Pensions, 401(k) and IRAs)

3 percent from assets (bank accounts and personal investments)

5 percent from other sources

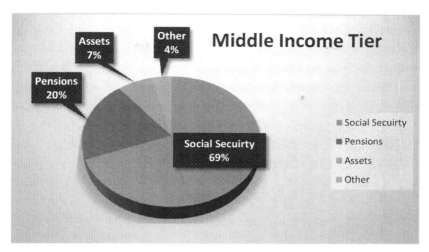

The Middle Income Tier: This represents the 33% of Americans 65 and older who make between $16,758 and $37,161 per year in 2009. They receive their retirement income from the same sources but with different percentages:

69 percent from Social Security

20 percent from pensions

7 percent from assets

4 percent from other sources

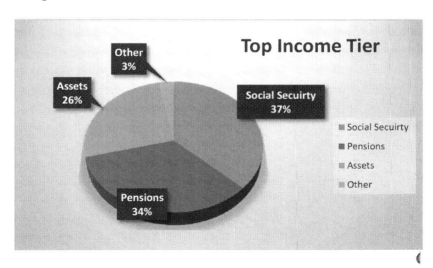

The Top Income Tier: This represents the final 33% of Americans 65 and over whose income is greater than $37,161 per year in 2009. Their income is more balanced between the main sources of retirement funds:

37 percent from Social Security
34 percent from pensions
26 percent from assets
3 percent from other sources[9]

## Determine Desired Income during Retirement

Every one of us dreams of having enough money when we retire. In fact, the majority (55%) of people working today are confident they will have enough to live comfortably throughout their retirement years.[10] This is an interesting conclusion since most people (more than 56%) have never even tried to estimate how much money they will actually need based upon projected living costs.

A big step you can take to prepare for your future and boost your confidence is to set a goal for how much income you would like to have during your retirement years. You, of course, can't predict with laser precision exactly what life will cost you but a common sense goal will add momentum to your plan. I don't know if you will be able to reach all your goals but I do know you will be more effective than if you don't set goals. Some of my favorite quotes on the value of having goals are:

*"Mistakes are always forgivable, if one has the courage to admit them" - Bruce Lee*[11]

*"Try not. Do or do not. There is no try." – Yoda in The Empire Strikes Back*[12]

*"If you don't know where you are going, you'll end up someplace else." – Yogi Berra*[13]

*"If you aim at nothing, you will hit it every time." – Zig Ziglar*[14]

To help you project the amount of income you want to have in the future, fill in the budget below. The categories in this budget are based on the Estimated Retirement Costs Worksheet in the Appendix section of this book. I think you will find it is well worth your time to put numbers to the desires in your heart so you can intelligently set goals for your retirement planning.

| The Life I Would Like to Afford in My Retirement | |
| --- | --- |
| Home Expenses | |
| Utilities | |
| Home Maintenence and Upkeep | |
| Food | |
| Transportation/Cars | |
| Charity | |
| Medical | |
| Personal Care | |
| Hobbies/Personal Development | |
| Family and Friends | |
| Personal Debt | |

| | |
|---|---|
| Taxes | |
| | |
| **The Goal I am Focused On:** | |

Now that you have your goal in mind, you can make plans with a purpose like the following two kids:

A police officer had found a perfect hiding place for identifying speeding motorists.

One day, the officer was amazed when everyone was under the speed limit, so he investigated and found the problem.

A 10 year old boy was standing on the side of the road with a huge hand painted sign which said "Radar Trap Ahead."

A little more investigative work led the officer to the boy's accomplice. Another boy was stationed about 100 yards beyond the radar trap with a sign that read "TIPS" and a bucket at his feet full of change.[15]

This is not a solid strategy for creating retirement income but it does demonstrate what can be accomplished when you have a clear goal!

*Chapter 5*

# IN SYNC WITH INFLATION

There are a few things in life I can guarantee with 100% certainty, such as, "You are going to get older" (sorry to have bring that up). None of us really like that news which is why we come up with humorous ways to deal with it. For instance, since short cuts have become so popular in texting and other social media, it is time to add some texting codes we can use once we retire:

CBM - Covered by Medicare
CUATSC - See You at the Senior Center
GHA - Got Heartburn Again
IMHO - Is My Hearing-Aid On?
LMDO - Laughing My Dentures Out
OMMR - On My Massage Recliner
OMSG - Oh My! Sorry, Gas
TTYL - Talk to You Louder
WAITT - Who Am I Talking To?[16]

Another promise I can make is that life will be more expensive in 10 years than it is today. This is what we affectionately call *inflation*. Just as putting air into a balloon causes it to inflate, adding time to economics causes prices to inflate. Some of you are thinking, *I have some things in my life that are way cheaper today than they were 10 years ago. Take my computer, for instance. When the personal computer was first introduced almost no one could afford one. Today, anyone who wants a computer can find a way to get one.* Of course you are right. Some individual products cost less but overall your life is more expensive today than it used to be and that will continue forever.

It isn't all bad news, however. As costs are going up, the average wage in America has also been rising. As a result, you have more to work with to address the fact that life is costing more. . In this case, deflation would not be your friend. We all saw recently that deflating footballs may make the ball easier to throw and catch but it can complicate your life for a long time![17] To illustrate the impact of inflation, let's take a stroll down memory lane and look at how things have changed.

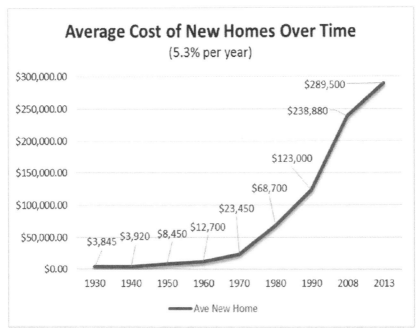

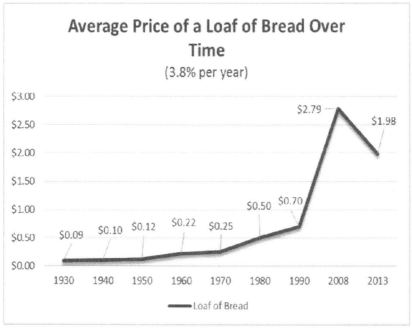

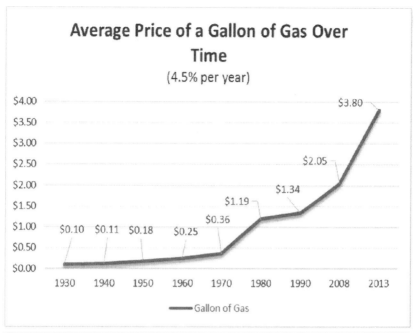

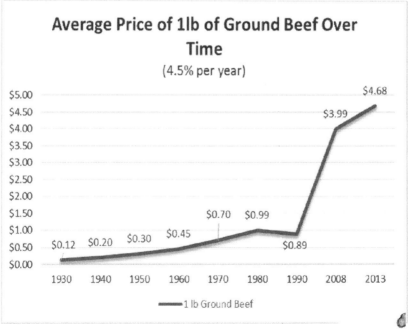

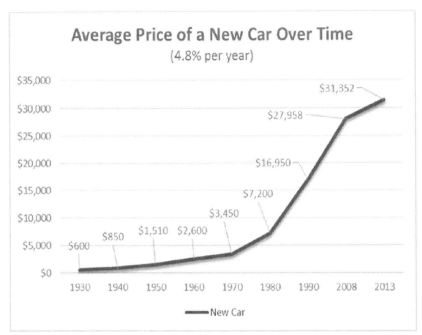

The previous examples only include 5 items from a typical American budget (home, car, bread, gas and ground beef). Although these are great things, your budget includes more than five things. When you combine everything involved in the U.S. economy, the inflation rate from 1913 to 2013 was 3.22%.[18] This is not bad while you are working because wages have generally kept up with the rise in costs. It is a major issue when you retire because your income tends to level off. It would be nice if businesses provided "retirement pricing" for all goods and services but we all know this is just a fantasy on par with romance novels and fairy tales - fun to dream about but quickly evaporates when you wake up.

In reality, life will cost more 10 years into retirement than the day you take the big step. Let me illustrate this with some numbers. Let's assume your house is paid for and you concluded your life would cost $25,000 the first year you retire. Assuming inflation holds at 3.22%, the exact same lifestyle would cost $34,322 10 years later. If you are fortunate to live another 10 years, you will need $47,121 if you made no other changes in the way you spend money. When you were making money, inflation helped you grow your income but when you retire, inflation is like a tire pump attached to your budget that causes every item to expand each and every year. The challenge is that the pump is not necessarily connected to your income!

### Getting Homey with Healthcare

And then there is healthcare. If medical issues have not been an issue for you, they most likely will be at some point during your retirement years. According to the Bureau of Labor Statistics, from 1982 to 2011, medical costs have risen at an average of 5.1% which you will notice is significantly higher than the 3.2% inflation rate that is typical in America.[19] Hopefully you will live long and experience great health. You can't budget with this mind, however. You must assume that your medical expenses will be larger in your seventies, eighties and beyond than at any other time in your life. Health Services Research conducted a study in 2004 to estimate how much health care will cost the average American and when they will spend that money. They discovered that the average American will spend $316,600 on healthcare throughout their lives and that almost 60% of that cost will be incurred after the age of 65.[20]

The United Health Foundation is a not-for-profit organization that is keeping track of the pulse of healthcare in the USA. Every year they research healthcare trends in the US and release their findings in two reports. An annual report which discusses what is happening in the general population and a senior report which focuses on the success and challenges of those 65 and older. In their 2013 senior report, they present information based on estimates of the Centers for Disease Control and Prevention that each of us ought to factor into our planning. When it comes to seniors in America (65 and older):

Nearly 8 in 10 are living with at least one chronic health condition and 50% have two or more.

About 25% are obese.

20% have been diagnosed with diabetes.

More than 70% have some form of heart disease.

Almost 60% have arthritis[21]

Nobody sets a goal to have these kinds of health challenges. It's hard to admit we have to wrestle with chronic health issues but the challenge seems easier if we are financially ready for them. Part of your future financial planning ought to, therefore, include a hefty amount for health and medical expenses. If you are one of the fortunate ones to experience good health for a long, long time, the money you have set aside for healthcare will make your retirement just a little more comfortable.

## Tackle the Tax Man

In addition to inflation, most people's tax strategy changes in retirement. The tax code assumes the average American will own a home and raise kids. Home ownership and family structures have historically been viewed as beneficial because they make our society stronger. Real estate is a vital part of the economy and families help develop character in their members and create a built-in restraint system so individuals make better choices. In recognition of their value to our culture, the IRS allows tax payers to deduct the interest portion of their mortgage from their taxable income and provides a deduction for each child in your home. Most retirees, however, have the goal of paying off their mortgage and helping their kids move out, which are great accomplishments that ought to be celebrated. When it comes to dealing with taxes, however, it seldom feels like accomplishments are celebrated. At some point in your life, you may have felt like George Pope who wrote the following letter to the IRS.

Dear Sir:

In reply to your request to send a check, I wish to inform you that the present condition of my bank account makes it almost impossible. My shattered financial conditions are due to Federal laws, corporation laws, mothers-in-law, brothers-in-law, sisters-in-law, and outlaws.

Through these taxes I am compelled to pay a business tax, assessment tax, head tax, school tax, income tax, casket tax, food tax, furniture tax, sales tax and excise tax. Even my brain is taxed.

I am required to get a business license, car license, hunting license, fishing license, truck and auto license, not to mention marriage and dog license. I am also required to contribute to every society and organization which the genius of man is capable of bringing into life; to women's relief, unemployed relief, and gold digger's relief. Also to every hospital and charitable institution in the city, including the Red Cross, the Black Cross, the Purple Cross and the Double Cross.

For my own safety, I am compelled to carry life insurance, liability insurance, burglary insurance, accident insurance, property insurance, business insurance, earthquake insurance, tornado insurance, unemployment insurance, old age insurance and fire insurance.

My own business is so governed that it is no easy matter for me to find out who owns it. I am inspected, suspected, disrespected, rejected, dejected, and compelled until I prove an inexhaustible supply of money for every known need of the human race.

Simply because I refuse to donate something or another I am boycotted, talked about, lied about, held up, held down and robbed until I am almost ruined. I can tell you honestly that except for a miracle that happened I could not enclose this check. The wolf that comes to my door nowadays just had pups in my kitchen. I sold them and here's the money.

Would like more business to pay more taxes.

Sincerely yours,
George Pope[22]


## Keep Inflation in Mind

Despite the regulations, taxes and rising costs, you are able to build for retirement because your income typically grows over the years as a result of inflation. It will be different in retirement but it doesn't have to be a bad thing. As you set goals for your future, keep in mind that inflation won't stop just because you stopped working! You simply need a new strategy that fits this season of your life.

*Chapter 6*

# EXECUTE YOUR PLAN

You may be asking at this point, how are others doing in their retirement? How much do other people make when they retire? The U.S. Census Bureau collected new data in 2012. Part of their findings show how much people are earning during their retirement years.[23]

| Yearly Income of Americans age 65 and older | |
| --- | --- |
| Less than $10,000 | 2% |
| $10,000 to $25,000 | 14% |
| $25,000 to $30,000 | 8% |
| $30,000 to $35,000 | 8% |
| $35,000 to $40,000 | 7% |
| $40,000 to $50,000 | 11% |
| $50,000 to $75,000 | 20% |
| $75,000 to $100,000 | 11% |
| $100,000 to $125,000 | 7% |
| $125,000 to $150,000 | 4% |
| $150,000 to $200,000 | 4% |
| Over $200,000 | 3% |

As you look at these figures, you are probably thinking about which category you would like to fit into. The good news is that people are figuring out how to make retirement work at a wide range of incomes. Your future years are very personal to you so I am confident you have a number in mind. You will not reach this number by accident so you will want to develop a strategy to turn your dream into a reality. An idea without a plan is nothing more than an empty dream. This is where your financial adviser comes into play. The questions you need to ask to create a strategy are straightforward:

What is my goal for my retirement income?

How much can I expect to receive from Social Security?

How much can I expect to receive from my pension?

How much will my 401(k) contribute to my future income?

How much will my IRA contribute to my retirement income?

How will my personal earnings and assets affect my retirement income?

Where should I invest my assets to insure a secure future income?

The answers to these questions, however, can be complex and surrounded by professional jargon. For instance, you may want to receive your pension in monthly payments or you may want to take a lump sum distribution and set up your own annuity. The calculations for this type of transaction are intricate and involve a number of governmental regulations. Your financial professional has spent his/her career investigating the options and can help you sort out what is best for you.

Set up an appointment with a qualified, dependable financial adviser and line out a strategy you can believe in.

## Execute Your Plan

Once you have your plan outlined, it is time to execute it. We all know people who have great intentions but never find the discipline to put feet to their plans. Exercise DVDs sit lifelessly on shelves. Diet plans were researched with sincerity but the daily action to make it work was swallowed up by fear, stress or the frantic pace of life. In the same way, many adults have outlined a financial plan for their retirement but then fail to translate it into a regular, disciplined series of actions.

An effective action plan will be

*Specific.* Few people have bad plans, but most people have plans that are too vague. Because they are vague, it is hard to focus on exactly what you are trying to accomplish. For instance:

Vague: "I will work hard my whole life," is a good desire  but it is too vague to know what it really means.

Specific: "I am going to work for 30 years with a goal of increasing my salary to $80,000 per year," is specific enough to understand.

Vague: "I will make contributions to my IRA each year," is a good idea but we still don't know what it means.

Specific: "I will put $4,000 per year in my IRA," is well-defined.

*Measurable*: Because this is an action plan, you need to be able to determine if your actions are working. When it comes to your future income, the measuring points are time and money. For every action step you write down, ask the following questions:

Is there a clear way to know if I have completed this step?

Is there a clear way to know when I have completed this step?

If someone else read this action step would they be able to tell when it was completed?

Example of an action step you can't measure: "I will change the amount of my paycheck going into my 401(k)." This is a good wish but there is no way to measure how much the amount will be or when the change will be made.

Example of an action step you can measure: "In March, I am going to increase my 401(k) deduction from $800 per month to $1,000 per month." This step has a clear time and dollar amount so you will know exactly if and when you have accomplished this step.

*Realistic*: It is great to have dreams but they must intersect with the reality of your life. You may want to save $50,000 toward your retirement this year but if you are earning $75,000 it is not realistic. It is certainly a great goal but you can frustrate yourself by outlining steps that are out of your reach. Small steps taken over time will be much more effective than big steps only dreamed about. So, recognize the value of the steps you can make and don't be discouraged by the steps you can't take yet.

*Seasonal:* The effectiveness of your choices will be determined by how well they fit into the season of life you are currently experiencing. Is it the planting season, growth season or harvest season of your financial life? The planting season calls for aggressive steps that have long-term potential for income development. The growing season calls for patient commitment to your investments. The harvesting season calls for strategic allocation of your resources so they provide safely and sufficiently for your needs. For example, 59 ½ and 70 ½ are strategic harvesting deadlines in your retirement planning that require informed decisions. A well-trained financial professional will understand why these dates are so important and should be able to give you wise guidance.

## Regularly Scheduled Reviews

The action steps you take to reach your goals are the yearly milestones that are building your future income. Each year, there are new possibilities, new challenges and new choices to be made. As your income grows, you can invest more. As your family grows, your joys and challenges multiply. Every year, your life changes physically, socially, intellectually and financially. To keep up with these changes, you will want to take a good look at your goals and the action steps that are driving them every year.

Choose the same time every year and put it on your calendar. Make an appointment with your financial adviser. It is a great time to get more information and to identify key decisions. It may seem a little intense if you are used to a more freewheeling approach but those who plan yearly have more confidence, less stress and less emotional turmoil in their family and their finances.

## Section 2

## YOU AND YOUR HOME

*Chapter 7*

# PROPERTY AND CASUALTY COVERAGE

Most people view their home as their greatest asset. In reality, your ability to earn an income is the largest asset in your life but your single most valuable possession is most likely going to be your house. You make bigger payments on your house than any other investment. You create bigger memories in your home than anywhere else. The market value of your property is only a share of its value because your house is a place where relationships are forged and decisions are worked out. These are the priceless activities of your life so it is virtually impossible to place a monetary value on them.

Something this important needs to be protected. My hope is that you never face a devastating event that needs to be covered by insurance. When a farmer erects a fence, he anticipates that it will stand forever. He doesn't think, this field will probably flood some day or it will probably catch fire some year which means I will have to replace this fence at some point in the future. He knows these perils may happen but he hopes they don't. He is smart enough to know that disasters are a part of life that are out of our control. He doesn't, however, assume they will happen.

In the same way, none of us anticipates that our home is going to be the one that gets vandalized or destroyed by an act of nature. In fact, it would be counterproductive for you to think this way. We all need to consider the possibilities but allowing yourself to become preoccupied with the negative possibilities of life will skew your attitude, raise your stress level and diminish your productivity. The following illustration is a good reminder.

A psychologist walked around a room while teaching stress management to an audience. As she raised a glass of water, everyone expected they'd be asked the "half empty or half full" question. Instead, with a smile on her face, she inquired, "How heavy is this glass of water?"

Answers called out ranged from 8 oz. to 20 oz.

She replied, "The absolute weight doesn't matter. It depends on how long I hold it. If I hold it for a minute, it's not a problem. If I hold it for an hour, I'll have an ache in my arm. If I hold it for a day, my arm will feel numb and paralyzed. In each case, the weight of the glass doesn't change, but the longer I hold it, the heavier it becomes."

She continued, "The stresses and worries in life are like that glass of water. Think about them for a while and nothing happens. Think about them a bit longer and they begin to hurt. And if you think about them all day long, you will feel paralyzed – incapable of doing anything."[24]

When it comes to preparing for the rare possibility of catastrophic perils, you basically have two options. You can save enough money to cover the cost of replacing your home, along with sufficient funds to cover any medical and legal bills that might accompany an unfortunate event. Or, you can purchase insurance.

Most of us cannot afford the first option so we choose to add insurance coverage as the fence that protects our home. What do you need to know about property and casualty coverage to help you make wise decisions?

### What is covered?

Typically, homeowners insurance will cover your house,

personal property inside the house and some form of personal liability. As you will quickly discover, everything in a homeowner's policy is defined. The coverage can be broken down into categories to help you better understand it.

Damage to the outside or inside of your house. When your home is damaged, your insurer will compensate you so that you can repair the structure or replace it in the case of total destruction. There are certain events that are covered while others are excluded. In the most common scenarios, the policy will cover damage from such perils as:

- A windstorm
- A hailstorm
- An aircraft accident
- A riot
- Vandalism
- A volcanic eruption
- An explosion
- A fire and/or smoke
- Lightening
- Rupture of a system in your home
- Falling objects
- Freezing of your plumbing

And the list goes on . . .

Certain perils will be excluded. The most common include:

- Earthquakes
- Floods
- Poor home maintenance
- Acts of war

Supplemental policies are available to cover earthquake and flood damage. If you live in a part of the country that is likely to face these challenges, you may want to add this fence to your insurance plan.

*Loss or damage to personal belongings.* Your home is more than just the walls, roof, windows and doors. It also includes your furniture, appliances, decorations, clothing and other possessions you have acquired over the years. If your home is destroyed, it is likely these will be lost also. You want your policy to allow you to go shopping for the possessions that matter most to you. "According to the Insurance Information Institute, most insurance companies will provide coverage for 50-70% of the amount of insurance you have on the structure of your home. If your house is insured for $200,000, there would be up to about $140,000 worth of coverage for your possessions."[25] As you shop for your insurance, you will need to decide if this is enough to cover the particular items you would want to replace. You can add more if you are willing to pay a higher premium but only you can make that decision.

*Personal liability.* It always possible that you, a member of your family or friends will cause damage to your home or get injured on your property. It may even be that your beloved pet breaks something significant or bites someone. You want to make sure you have sufficient coverage to address doctor visits, hospital treatment and possible loss of income. Policies generally start at $100,000 of coverage but "most experts recommend having at least $300,000 worth of coverage."[26]

*Rental of a residence while your home is being rebuilt or repaired.* This provision of homeowner's policies is seldom needed but if you are displaced because of damages, you will conclude it is brilliant to have this in your policy. This provision will reimburse you for the cost of rent, hotel costs, some meal costs and other incidental expenses you incur because you cannot live in your home. These provisions tend to be outlined in detail in your policy so review them before you begin spending money following a disaster. Your agent will probably be of great help at this point since it may be hard to think clearly at that moment.

### Reasons for Having Homeowner's Insurance

There are a number of reasons why you want to have homeowner's insurance. "Virtually all mortgage lenders require insurance coverage to protect their investment."[27] Whatever mortgage company you decided to go with when you bought your home, they have invested a lot of money into your house. For a long time, they are the "real owners" of the place you call home. As you continue to make payments, you have the hope that one day you will be given the deed to the property and it will truly be yours. Until that day, however, you are in a joint venture and the bank holds the primary position. If something were to happen and your house was either damaged or destroyed, the mortgage holder would suffer a large financial loss. As a result, they will most likely require you to carry a policy as a condition of the loan.

You have more personal reasons than protecting the bank, however, to carry a property and casualty policy. This is your home. It is the place where you build memories, forge character, relieve stress and operate from as your base of operations. You rely on your home and you find strength from calling a place your own. If something were to happen, it could be devastating to you financially, emotionally and relationally. Nobody wants to even think about their house being destroyed by fire, wind, hurricanes or anything else. It will, however, give you peace of mind if you know you can replace your home if the unthinkable did happen.

You probably also like to invite people to your home. Friends add value to your life and help you feel like your life matters. Hosting family gatherings helps you build traditions and solidify the most enduring relationships of your life. Inviting acquaintances provides the opportunity to build new friendships.

Each of these activities are great but they are also risky. Anytime you have people visit your property, there is a possibility that someone will get hurt. I never want you to plan your events with this in mind but I also don't want you to be naïve about the possibility. Having an insurance policy that covers you against liability, allows you to relax with your guests knowing you are covered.

**All Insurance is NOT Created Equal**

You will notice that different homeowner's policies have different costs associated with them. In simple terms, the more coverage you would like on your property the more you will pay for your policy. As you talk with your agent about your insurance, you will hear about three levels of coverage you can choose from:

1. Actual cash value. In this scenario, the company will cover your house plus the value of your belongings after deducting for depreciation. That is a big word that may or may not make sense to you. Without going into too much detail, this means the insurer will reimburse you based on what the items are worth today, not how much you paid for them when you first bought them.

2. Replacement cost. This is the actual cash value of your possessions without deducting for depreciation. In other words, you would be able to repair or rebuild your home up to its original value.

3. Guaranteed replacement cost. This is the most comprehensive coverage you can get which will account for inflation. Simply stated, this coverage pays whatever it actually costs to repair or rebuild your home, even if it costs more than your policy limits.

**How Much Does Homeowner's Insurance Cost**

This is generally the first question that comes to mind when we think about getting insurance. It is an important question because none of us (well, at least most of us) have unlimited budgets so we must be conscious of our commitments. This is a hard question to answer, however. It is similar to asking, "How much does a car cost?" The answer is, "It depends on facts and circumstances." The fact is you want to buy a car. The circumstances include the type of car you purchase, the options you decide to have included and the willingness of the seller to negotiate. These all contribute to the cost of a car. In similar fashion, there are many factors that contribute to the price and value of the policies that are available to you. Factors that affect the cost of your policy include but are not limited to:

- The replacement cost of your home.
- A household inventory to determine the value of your contents.
- The amount of liability protection you choose.
- Your zip code – crime statistics tend to impact insurance costs.
- Number of claims filed against the house in the past.
- Proximity to fire hydrants and other fire prevention measures.
- Amount of the deductible you choose.

Another important factor in the cost of your policy is the company you choose. There is a highly competitive market out there so there are lots of options for you to choose from. It is in your best interest to do some comparison shopping or work with an agent who will show you multiple quotes from multiple companies and help you evaluate which fits your needs the best.

**A Note about Public Adjusters**
Any claim you make on your policy is going to be

a negotiation. The insurance company wants to figure out what is fair for them to pay. You want to figure out what is fair for you to receive. The insurance company is going to have adjusters on staff who will assess the damage, review the evidence involved and determine how much they believe you are entitled to. Because they are hired by the insurance company, they are going to look for a balance between your best interests and the company's.

In a major claim, you may want to have an adjuster who is representing you. This is where public adjusters come into play. A public adjuster is a professional you can employ to do an independent review of your losses, compile evidence related to your case, certify the value of your possessions and create well-designed reports to submit to your insurance company to help you receive the most equitable settlement possible.

When your home suffers major damage, it is highly emotional for you. You and your family members will be in shock and you will likely grieve over the loss of sentimental keepsakes. You will also probably be overwhelmed by the prospect of rebuilding and somehow replacing priceless family memories. While you are on this emotional rollercoaster, you are supposed to think clearly about the business of settling your claim. It is a huge understatement to say that this is a challenge. You are trying not be devastated while you are required to be efficient and thorough. A competent public adjuster can ease the burden by doing much of this work for you.

Public adjusters are most useful after an unfortunate peril to make sure your property is restored to its pre-loss condition, but they can also be useful long before. Since they don't work for the insurance company, they can help you assess the best coverage for your home and its contents. They can help think through the level of coverage that makes sense for your investment and create a thorough inventory of your possessions. Since they are not emotionally attached to everything in your home, they can create a more objective and realistic inventory. In most cases, their assessment will yield a higher value because they see things you miss and find value in items you have long since taken for granted.

In my opinion, the best public adjusters will have the following minimum characteristics:

- They are licensed in your state.
- They are bonded in your state.
- They receive their payment from your settlement. This means you will not be required to pay them up front. They will receive a percentage of the settlement they help you negotiate so it is a win-win scenario.

The fact that you are reading this book means you are an interested, thinking individual. You have probably asked, therefore, why would I need a public adjuster when I have an insurance agent? The reason is simple – experience. If you experience a catastrophic loss with your property, it will probably (and hopefully) be the only time it happens. You will have to learn how to assess your property, inventory your possessions and create reports "on the job." Adjusters work with these procedures year after year. They have seen this before and have become proficient at the process. As a result, they can help you perform better than you normally would, thus reducing stress and helping you to operate with more confidence.

If you are interested in working with a public adjuster, feel free to contact me for a referral. You will find my contact information in the back of the book.

*Chapter 8*

# CONSIDER A
# PUBLIC ADJUSTER

Sometimes working with your homeowner's insurance company is a great experience. Your agent and other representatives can be informed and remarkably cooperative in helping you understand your coverage and settling a claim. In these cases, it is like a tall glass of iced tea on a warm summer afternoon.

Sometimes, the same experience can be like the following scenario that took place on the golf course:

After a particularly bad round of golf, Robert decided not to go to the nineteenth hole [the clubhouse bar] and started to go straight home. As he was walking to the golf car park to get his Range Rover, a policeman stopped him and asked', Did you tee off on the seventeenth hole about twenty minutes ago?'

'Yes', Robert answered

'Did you happen to slice your ball so that it went over the trees and out of bounds and completely off the golf course?'

'Yes, I did. How did you know?' Robert questioned.

'Well', said the policeman gravely', Your golf ball flew out onto the main road and crashed through the windscreen of a BMW. The car driver lost control and crashed into six other cars and a fire engine. The fire engine was unable to reach the fire in time and the building burned down. Now, what do you intend to do about it?'

Robert thought it over very carefully and responded, "I think

I'll close my stance a little bit, tighten my grip and lower my right thumb."[28]

A conversation was had, the description of the scene was accurate but it ended with a confusing and disturbing response.

It can be the same way with an insurance claim. Insurance companies tend to speak a different language than the typical homeowner. In an oversimplified way it can be said that insurers focus on the peril that causes damage while homeowners tend to focus on the damage itself. It is vital, therefore, that any claim you submit to your insurance company is written in the language of the policy rather than the language of your heart. Consider the following two scenarios:

*Scenario 1:* Peter and Alicia discovered a wet area under their refrigerator. Instinctively, they called their insurance agent to report the incident. The agent was kind and patiently listened to his clients. At the end of the meeting he told them, "I will pass the information on to our adjuster who will be contacting you to go over the case and work things out."

The adjuster, like the agent, was kind and considerate over the phone. She explained that she would be asking a few questions and would contact a restoration company on their behalf. After the introduction, she sincerely asked, "So, what happened?"

Peter took the lead and said, "I walked into my kitchen and noticed water on my tile floor. It got my attention because it squished under my feet. The water ran over into the dining room that has a hardwood floor. I went downstairs and could see water dripping through the floor. It was getting both my treadmill and sofa wet. Now our basement is 'flooded' and it looks like it's been leaking for a really long time because some of framing has mold growing on it."

The adjuster thanked Peter for the information and signed off with a simple, "OK, I've got it."

The couple was impressed with the way the adjuster

listened over the phone so they were glad to see the restoration company show up at their door with a clipboard and a camera. They showed the representative around so he could take pictures of the damage. You can imagine their disappointment when they were told, "The insurance company asked me to come see you but you should know they will not pay for the damage. They have determined it was caused by neglect rather than a peril."

Peter and Alicia got a hard lesson in how insurance actually works. The company does not cover "damage" even though the average homeowner thinks they do. The company covers "perils" as outlined in the policy. To qualify as a peril, an event must be something that happens accidentally and suddenly. When Peter mentioned his basement was "flooded," the insurance company had a way of denying the claim. In addition, the description that "it looks like it has been leaking for a really long time," took the claim out of the category of being sudden. Peter was trying to be honest and transparent but never meant to disqualify his claim.

*Scenario 2:* Peter and Alicia discovered a wet area under their refrigerator. They decided to call a public adjuster at the encouragement of a friend. The public adjuster was focused and informed and took time to explain to the couple how the insurance company would process their claim. They were a little nervous when he asked to see their homeowner's policy, but calmed down when he explained that their claim would need to be written in the language of their policy if it was to have a good chance of being honored. He also explained that the claim may take a little longer to settle because we will need to document everything carefully. I want you to know up front that I will only get paid if we successfully get you a settlement.

The public adjuster called the agent to introduce himself and let him know he would be representing Peter and Alicia. He then said they would be submitting a written description of the event.

The public adjuster's description included the following, "An accidental discharge of water was found in the residence. Damage was discovered in the kitchen, dining room and basement. The policy holders do not know how long water has been discharging because it was not obvious. They just became aware of the issue."

The adjuster from the insurance company came by the house to investigate. She documented the extent of the damage and confirmed Peter and Alicia were not aware of the problem until just recently. She then told them she would be submitting her report and would contact a restoration company if they wanted. They told her they already had a restoration company lined up and thanked her for the visit.

The couple was relieved when their public adjuster came by the house to announce the insurance company was going to cover the damage, provide them with temporary housing while the repairs were being made and their damaged furniture would be replaced.

Peter and Alicia were amazed at how powerful words are in negotiating an insurance claim. As homeowners, they don't speak the language of insurance and would not have thought on their own to put their claim in terms that coincide with their policy. Their public adjuster, on the other hand, had the experience and training to know how to speak the language that brought legitimate results.

## The Process of Filing a Claim

When you suffer damage from an unexpected accident or peril, you have the right to submit a claim to your insurance company. This is, as a matter of fact, the reason you purchased insurance in the first place. You hoped you would never have to use it but you wanted to have it in place just in case.

The first step in filing a claim is contacting the

company that issued the policy. You can do this yourself or you can hire a public adjuster to represent you. Either way, the claim process is initiated by you in response to an event that causes damage to your home.

When a claim is made, the insurance company will go through a process to assess the damage and determine the level of their liability. The process will include the following basic steps:

- The company will review the policy to determine whether the loss is covered. Policies are written in specific terms that outline what is covered and what is excluded. They will only commit to pay for damages caused by covered events.
- The company will investigate the type and extent of damage to determine the company's liability.
- The company will then estimate the amount of compensation to be paid based upon the determined liability.

If and when the company determines they will pay to repair the damaged property they may allow you to choose your own contractors or they may suggest companies they prefer to work with, or a combination of the two.

Although the company has a system they follow, every aspect of the claim is negotiable. The insurance company will attempt to minimize the amount they pay out. I think we all understand this because the insurance company wants and needs to make money to stay in business. They will, therefore, seek to maximize their bottom line. As a homeowner, you want to make sure that all damages are covered so your home will be fully functional when the work is finished. You can, therefore, negotiate with your insurer or hire a public adjuster to represent you in the settlement.

If, in the process, you disagree with the offer from the insurance company, you have a few options:

- You can enter mediation with a neutral third party. This third party is trained in leading mediated settlements and will help facilitate an agreement. This agreement, however, is non-binding in a legal sense and is solely based on the mutual agreement of the parties involved.

- You can enter an appraisal process which also involves a third party who facilitates an agreement. An appraisal will produce a binding dispute resolution which must be honored by both sides.
- You can enter litigation where a binding resolution is reached through the court system by negotiation or trial.

**Why is it called Adjusting?**

The process of investigating a claim to determine the insurance company's liability is called adjusting. The case will be looked at in detail to determine the extent of the damage which will then be "adjusted" to reflect the amount the company is liable for and how much will be the owner's responsibility. There are three types of adjusters who may be involved in any insurance claim:

1. Company adjusters who work directly for the insurance company.
2. Independent adjusters who contract with insurance companies to provide adjusting services.
3. Public adjusters who work for the policyholder in settling claims.

As you see from the list above, the company will have at least one adjuster on the case who will be looking out for the insurer's interest in the claim. In most cases, homeowners trust these services and believe the process is above board and sincerely aimed at helping the homeowner. Public adjusters are available to the homeowner who would like to have a representative involved in the case whose main focus is to look out for the interests of the policyholder.

When a public adjuster is involved, the claim tends

to take longer to resolve. This makes sense because more people are scrutinizing the claim and more negotiating will take place before a settlement is reached. At the same time, claims tend to be settled for larger amounts when a public adjuster is employed. This is partly due to a fuller investigation and addressing of the problems with the result that damages are addressed thoroughly. It is also due to the inclusion of the public adjuster fee. In most cases, the net amount you will receive as a policyholder will be larger when a public adjuster is involved.

## Preventative Medicine

Mandy Hale in her book The Single Woman: Life, Love, and a Dash of Sass writes, "What we are waiting for is not as important as what happens to us while we are waiting. Trust the process." [29] This is good advice when it comes to homeowner's insurance. Your success in settling a claim if the need arises will be based on the wisdom you employed when you chose your insurance coverage. A public adjuster can be a great help in this regard. Because the adjuster understands the language of the policy and has experience submitting and verifying claims, he or she has keen insight into the type of coverage your particular dwelling ought to have. Before you commit to your property and casualty insurance, consider having a public adjuster survey your property and make recommendations on the type and scope of coverage you would benefit from the most.

## Opinions are Divided

As you can imagine, insurance companies and public adjusters have different opinions about the role and impact of having a public adjuster involved in your claim. Some of the significant opinions include:

Insurance Companies say:

- Public adjusters insulate policyholders from insurance companies and create distrust between the insurance company and the policyholder.
- Public adjusters increase the time to settle claims when they make it difficult for insurance companies to schedule inspections and meet with policyholders and make it necessary for insurance companies to spend additional time investigating and verifying damage estimates provided by public adjusters.
- Company adjusters should have the opportunity to settle claims with policyholders before public adjusters get involved.
- Public adjusters utilize misleading advertising to solicit business with policyholders.
- Public adjusters make it difficult for policyholders to make all repairs included in the claim because a portion of the settlement amount goes to the public adjuster.
- Public adjusters increase the cost of insurance for all consumers.

In contrast, public adjusters say:

- Public adjusters are the only advocates that exclusively represent the policyholder.
- Insurance companies impose too much burden on policyholders to prove their claims.
- Insurance companies are not motivated to provide full compensation to the policyholder since their responsibility is to their shareholders.
- Insurance companies cause delays in settling claims due to poor communication; failure to respond to requests in a timely manner; and excessive demands for documentation.[30]

**It's Your Choice**

It is up to you whether you want to use the services of a public adjuster or not. It is my opinion that you will get a more accurate assessment of damages and more effectively settle your claim if you utilize one of these trained professionals. If you are looking for a referral in your area to a certified public adjuster, visit my website or contact my office. (You will find the contact information at the back of the book)

*Chapter 9*

# REVOCABLE LIVING TRUSTS

L ike many of you, I have had a variety of career pursuits in my lifetime. As a young adult, I spent time as a Navy Corpsman. The work suited me well for a number of different reasons. Having been raised in a farming community, I was comfortable with the realities of injuries, infections and other maladies. As a compassionate man, I found it satisfying to help people heal and find a sense of peace in the midst of difficulty. As a man who is interested in spiritual things, I found it rewarding to comfort people as they faced the inevitable.

It was amazing how many people would talk to me openly and candidly when they came to the realization that their days on earth were just about done.

"Mark, I have farmland in Indiana that has been in my family for years. I would like this land to go to my oldest son. I never told him that I wanted him to have the land because I thought I had plenty of time. He is only 11 years-old so I didn't think it was time. Can you make sure my wife and son know this is what I want done? I am counting on you, Mark."

"Thanks for all the help you've given me, Mark. I hate to ask you this but I guess I need to tell someone. I put some gold in a safe deposit box years ago. I never told anyone about it. Anyway, I would really like my brother to be the recipient of the coins. Can you tell him for me?"

"Well, Mark, I didn't think I would have to face this but I figure I don't have too many more days. I always thought there was time to make plans but here I am. I don't have a lot but I do want my wife to get control of the house, the bank accounts and the rental property I have. Can you see what you can do to make that happen?"

I could go on because almost everyone wants to talk to whoever is close by when they realize they may not have much time. I think of myself as a good guy so I did my best to honor these sincere requests. In almost every situation, however, I was disappointed. The requests were sincere. My motivation was sincere. My conversations with the family members were sincere. The results, however, were awkward because very few of these families had paperwork in place to facilitate the desires of their hearts. I wasn't officially authorized to represent them so my words didn't hold much weight. The families hadn't planned ahead because their loved ones were healthy and relatively young.

Talking with these family members was like riding a rollercoaster. When they heard the desire of their loved one to pass on assets to them, they were touched by the gesture and relieved by the help it would provide. As they began to process the request and ran into roadblocks, they would grow frustrated and angry. All I could do was watch them take this emotional ride because the tools were not in place.

This is why I am a fan of revocable living trusts.

## What is a Revocable Living Trust?

A revocable living trust is an estate planning tool that allows you to determine how your property and other assets will be passed on to others. Although many legal documents can have confusing names, each word in revocable living trust is significant.

*Revocable.* Most living trusts are "revocable" because they can be changed during your lifetime. If your circumstances change, your collection of assets changes or your wishes call for a modification, you have the ability to rewrite the provisions of your trust.

*Living.* The trust is considered "living" because you create it during your lifetime. It represents your wishes and plans while you are alive and in full control of your faculties.

*Trust.* It is a document signed by you and a notary public so it represents a trustworthy report of your wishes.

## The Benefits of a Revocable Living Trust

Avoid Probate. Most people use living trusts to avoid probate. My guess is you have heard that statement before but you probably don't know what probate is. In simple terms, "probate is the court-supervised process of wrapping up a person's estate."[31] Probate means "to prove" and requires you to show evidence to a judge that the assets of your loved one belong to you. As a result, the assets are put in public records so that others can attempt to prove they should receive a portion of the distribution. Most people find this process to be dissatisfying because the court, by its very nature, approaches your estate without feeling or personal motivation. As a result, probate can be expensive as lawyers have to get involved to settle your assets. It can be time consuming because many people are going to want to get in on the action. The government will seek what it believes it is entitled to. Creditors will want to make sure they get their cut. Your loved ones will brings their hopes to the discussion. Others may unexpectedly show up making a claim to your family's assets. As a result, probate tends to be a burden to the ones you love most in life.

Officially identify Beneficiaries. In your trust, you can itemize your property and other assets and assign them to the beneficiaries you want. All property you have assigned will then pass to your beneficiaries without probate.

## How do I set up a Trust?

Although you could set up a trust document on your own, it is advisable to work with an Elder Estate Attorney who is trained in setting up revocable living trusts. If you need a referral, feel free to contact me (my contact information is in the back of the book). The process of creating a trust will include the following minimum steps:

- A trust document is created – usually from a template.
- The trust is given a name.
- A trustee is named (usually you). This is the person who will take care of the property in the trust.
- The property covered by the trust is itemized in a list. Most of your assets can simply be listed but any titled property (such as real estate) must be retitled in the name of the trust to make sure it is included. If not, it could end up in probate.
- The person (or people) who will get the property when the trust maker passes away are named in the document.
- A successor trustee is named who will take over after the trust maker's death.

Once all this information is written into the trust, the document is signed by the trust maker and verified by a notary public.

## What is the difference between a Revocable Living Trust and a Will?

Most trusts will include a will in the trust package because they both serve useful purposes in your estate planning. There are some similarities but they each have some unique capabilities. It is kind of like comparing a car to a pickup truck. They both drive on the road. They both will transport passengers. They can both get groceries from the store. Trucks can do some things, however, that cars can't do. For instance, they haul loads much better than cars do. I would hate to pick up a small load of hay in my car! On the other hand, cars tend to be more comfortable for passengers and usually get better gas mileage. They are built differently because they do different things.

Both wills and trusts can accomplish the following outcomes for you:

- Name beneficiaries for your property
- Leave property to young children, and
- Revise your document as your circumstances or wishes change.

A trust will accomplish the following outcomes that a will cannot:

- Avoid probate.
- Reduce the chance of a court dispute over your estate.
- Avoid a conservatorship. This is a condition in which a guardian and protector is assigned by a judge to manage your financial affairs because of limitations due to physical ailments, mental incapacitation or old age.
- Keep your document private after death. This can be especially attractive since the provisions of your trust are not public documents like your will would be during probate.

A will allows you to accomplish the following outcomes that a trust cannot:

- Name guardians for children.
- Name managers for children's property.
- Name an executor, and
- Instruct how debts or taxes should be paid.[32]

### Power of Attorney

In my opinion, one element you want to include in your trust is a durable power of attorney. "A durable power of attorney lets you arrange for someone you choose, called your 'attorney-in-fact', to manage your finances."[33] Your power of attorney can be made effective immediately or it can be engaged by a triggering event. For instance, you can assign the power of attorney to go into effect if you have a debilitating illness or accident or if a health professional determines you are no longer able to make sound decisions. You can also include a medical power of attorney to give legal authority to your attorney-in-fact to make medical decisions on your behalf. A competent trust lawyer can help you put these in place to insure your desires are not only communicated but empowered.

# Section 3

## TYPES OF INVESTORS

*Chapter 10*

# YOUR INVESTOR STYLE

No matter who you are, you are attached to money. It is the fuel in the tank of life that allows everything else to work. It can't buy true friends, make you happy or dictate the attitudes of your loved ones. But you can't operate your life without it. When you believe you have enough money, you tend to relax and focus on important priorities that give your life meaning and satisfaction. When you feel you don't have enough, your stress level rises and your focus gets riveted on your finances. In other words, we all have an emotional attachment to our money and we all have opinions about its value and role in our lives.

*Money is only a tool. It will take you wherever you wish, but it will not replace you as the driver.* - Ayn Rand[34]

*Recession is when a neighbor loses his job. Depression is when you lose yours.* - Ronald Reagan[35]

*"A simple rule dictates my buying: Be fearful when others are greedy, and be greedy when others are fearful."* Warren Buffet[36]

Despite its limitations, the need for money is real. We are all responsible to make a living during our productive years. Wisdom also declares that we ought to invest a portion of the money we earn to prepare for the future. I wish it were as simple as putting together a math problem where you save the same amount of money every month, place it in a solid investment without disturbing it and then reap the benefits when you retire. Unfortunately, few of us are this simple and straightforward when it comes to investing our finances.

## The Starting Point

Based upon your temperament, life experiences and natural confidence level, you have a home base for your approach to making investments. This is your basic style that defines how you think about money and how you like to approach investing. It is the way you would manage your investments every time if you had control over the forces that impact your finances. To gain a working knowledge of your home base, let's compare it to the way people drive. Every time you venture out on the road, you encounter various types of drivers. Some of the drivers are cautious and seem to have safety as their primary concern. Others are risk-takers who seem to think every road is a race track. If you are like most, you have developed attitudes about the way people drive. Evidence of this can be seen in the abundance of bumper stickers. Some of my favorite are:

> Experience is what you get when you don't get what you want.
> Hang up and drive!
> I don't suffer from insanity, I enjoy every minute of it

As you read through each of these, ask yourself which one comes closest to the way you like to operate.

***The Commuter.*** This is the largest group. These are conservative investors who are patient and steady and prefer to invest in the "sure" thing. In driving, commuters follow the same route every day. They leave at the same time, drive roughly the same speed on each trip and know how long it takes to get from home to work. They adjust to changing conditions but don't like it because they know how people ought to drive this route. They thrive on the routine and love the predictability of following the same driving routine each day.

When it comes to investing, the Commuter is drawn to the "sure" thing. They like predictable investments, guaranteed returns and low risk ventures. They are probably missing out on gains that someone else is going to benefit from but they take comfort in the fact that they are not going to get sideswiped by an out of control investment.

***The Off-Roader***. Some drivers need to go where others fear. They seek out new roads, crave intense challenges and like the "rough texture" of unpaved trails. In driving, they are fun to be around and adventurous.

Investments for the Off-Roader are adventures waiting to be experienced. They are drawn to new, innovative, "on the move" companies and thrive on the risk that may result in big gains or spectacular mishaps. Most people tell these investors to "stay off that road," "don't go there," or "I would never venture down that path." Off-Roaders, however, have a vibrant need to take the risk and see how it turns out.

***The Collector***. Some people simply love cars. They like to have a car for work, a car for the weekend, cars that remind them of their past and vehicles that add character to life. They usually own numerous cars at any one time and will trade cars often to keep the experience alive.

When it comes to finances, the Collector will employ a number of different strategies. Collectors utilize different approaches for different risk levels and like to have a balance of secure investments and risky pursuits. The one thing all these investments have in common is the Collector "likes" them or is comfortable with them. In the same way that car collectors acquire vehicles that are fascinating, investment collectors fill their portfolios with investments that interest them.

***The Passenger***. Some people would rather ride in the passenger seat than drive. They believe others are better drivers and feel more secure when others have the wheel.

When it comes to investing, Passengers do what others tell them to do. They are generally undereducated about or disinterested in financial strategies. If you are a Passenger at heart, you will seek out others you personally trust and do what you are advised to do. Even when you are challenged to think for yourself, you find greater comfort in following the lead of others who are more interested and confident than you.

*The GPS Follower.* Some drivers love the presence of a GPS in their cars. They never memorize routes or look up directions because their GPS will always lead them where they need to go. When the GPS Follower gets in the driver's seat, he immediately consults his trusted navigation system even if he has driven the route numerous times.

In investing, the GPS Follower seeks out trusted professionals who are skilled in their field. They won't take the advice of just anyone because they want their leaders to have the proper credentials. They tend to be busy and focused people who do not want to take a lot of time researching information that others already know.

*The First Responder.* Some drivers make a living solving problems. They drive quickly to the scene of a crime or an accident to do the work others are unwilling to perform. The very situations that tend to overwhelm others draw them like a magnet.

When it comes to investing, First Responders see great opportunity in the problems others have created. They look for companies that have been mishandled in order to rescue them. They seek out investments with great potential that have been misjudged by previous investors. They are adventurous, bold and well-informed. They also have unusual instincts for recognizing investments that can be turned around.

### Beware of the Force

Each of the base styles of investing have merit and will work for the individual who embraces the associated implications. Each style has a logical foundation and rational reasons for the way it operates. Decisions, however, are not limited to logic. There are many forces that affect the outcome of our choices. An example from history involves the question, "Why is the gauge (length between the tracks) of railroad tracks 4 feet, 8½ inches?" It is an interesting question because it seems odd. Why not 4 feet, 6 inches or 5 feet, which would seem more logical?

The reason begins with the English who began developing train technology before the Americans. When English engineers initiated their design, they used current transportation technologies as a guide rather than start from scratch. The current technology consisted of horse-drawn tramways which was now to be replaced with the iron horse. The gauge of the tramways in the early 1800s was based on the width of 2 horses which were used to pull the carts. As far back as the Roman Empire, it was determined that the equivalent of 4 feet 8½ inches was the strategic size between wheels on a chariot that was pulled by 2 horses. That length was passed on throughout European history to England. When Americans became interested in trains, the original U.S. railroad companies ordered equipment from England.

Americans, however, are innovators so the value of train transportation gave rise to many railroad operations. These companies experimented with several different gauges. Companies in the northern states stuck with the English track size while several companies in the southern states used sizes ranging from 2 feet to 6 feet. When the Civil War broke out, the North was able to move equipment and troops more efficiently than the South because of the standard size of their rail equipment. This was one of the primary reasons the North was victorious. After the Civil War, the standardization of the northern railroad took over the southern states creating a standard gauge throughout the country. If the South had won, it is quite possible the size of the tracks would be different today.

The idea of developing a rail system was brilliant and logical. The process of developing the technology, however, was deeply affected by issues that have little to do with trains. Horse transportation, the human tendency to copy existing designs and the outcome of the most intense war in American history all contribute to the modern state of railroads.[37]

In the same way, our financial decisions start out as logical, rational expressions of our preferred style of investing. It doesn't take long, however, before those decisions are affected by emotional factors in our lives. Before we take a look at these emotional winds that sway our financial choices, identify your base investing style. The styles are listed in the chart below so you can mark (with an "X" in the first column) the one that best fits your preference.

| My Investing Style | | |
|---|---|---|
| | *Commuter* | Conservative, patient, steady, likes the "sure" thing. |
| | *Off-Roader* | Drawn to new, innovative, "on the move" companies and thrive on risk |
| | *Collector* | Utilize different strategies for different risk levels, likes to balance secure investments with risky ventures. |
| | *Passenger* | Seek out others they trust personally and do what they are advised to do. |

| | | |
|---|---|---|
| | *GPS Follower* | Busy, seek out trusted professionals who are skilled In their field. Only listen to people who well versed in finances. |
| | *First Responder* | Adventurous, bold and well-informed. See great opportunity in the problems that others have created. |

Rely on your style because it is part of who you are. It is reliable and effective in giving you confidence for your choices. When you discover that you are valuable and talented, it is amazing what you can accomplish. In the same way, the ability to figure out investments that work for you is already within you. As you identify your style, you may just surprise yourself with newfound confidence!

# Chapter 11

# THE W.I.N.D.S. THAT BLOW

Fences would be easier to maintain if the weather was always mild. The climate, however, is ever changing. The wind blows with the rain, snow and sleet. As the winds blow, the posts, slats and wire can be broken, bent and damaged. The wise farmer will, therefore, build his fences to withstand the weather and will inspect them after a significant storm.

In the same way, investing would be much simpler if we consistently made financial decisions according to our investing style. We are, however, more complex than this. When your vehicle heads out on the highway, you are subject to prevailing weather conditions. At times, the weather is mild and has little impact on your driving decisions. Other days usher in light breezes with occasional gusts that cause you to make adjustments but they are so slight you hardly notice. Then there are the stormy days

that hinder your progress and raise your fears. In similar fashion there are emotional winds that blow in our lives when it comes to money that can affect the financial fences we have set up . The winds consist of:

## Whims

We pride ourselves on being rational, logical beings. While it is certainly true that much of our lives is guided by sound reasoning, we are not purely rational in our important decisions. Mixed with sage thoughts are approaches to financial decisions that can only be described as whims of the heart rather than wisdom of the mind.

The most common is the tendency for men and women to create emotional categories for money based on where the funds came from and what the money will be used for. For example:

- Income from your salary is viewed differently than a gift your grandparents gave you for your birthday.
- Money you have listed in your budget to pay bills is treated differently than money you are putting away for vacation.
- You may be diligently saving money for your kids' education while you are barely making minimum payments on your credit card debt.

If you had a purely logical approach to finances, there would be no difference between money you received from a salary or from a gift. Money is money no matter where it comes from. There would also be no difference between money designated for bills or set aside for vacation. You would have one budget that balances income with expenses. Logic would also demand that you pay off high interest credit cards before saving money in a lower interest investment. We maintain these emotional categories because they make us feel better, help lower stress and give expression to our relational priorities.

Another common whim that captures people's

attention is the balance of choices. When a person is presented with a short list of choices, they tend to choose the option that is in the "middle." Imagine you were handed a dinner menu at one of your favorite restaurants. On the menu are three options for the main entree. One costs $12, another costs $17 and the third costs $22. Most people will choose the $17 option simply because it is in the middle. Interestingly, when people are presented with too many options, they tend to do nothing. They get overwhelmed with the possibilities, become emotionally flooded and respond to the felt need to get out of the situation. The overwhelming volume of choices throws the process out of balance causing decision-making paralysis.

From a logical point of view, being "in the middle" means nothing. It says nothing about the quality of the choice, the value it will produce or the effectiveness of the investment. Similarly, a long list of choices does not affect the quality of the choices. Each possibility stands on its own merit regardless of how many options exist. And yet, we seem to think clearer when there is a balance that feels good to us.

## Independence

One of the great things about human beings is our belief that we are right most of the time. Sure it can get us in trouble but it also leads to confidence and boldness. Our self-confident independence leads us to approach decisions with preconceived notions. We naturally filter all new information through these tightly held biases. If a new piece of information agrees with our assumptions, we tend to think it is good information. If the information does not sync up with our notions, we reject it as worthless or meaningless. We do this for emotional reasons because we don't want to do the hard work of adjusting our thinking except when absolutely necessary. We want to believe there are some things in life that remain constant and can be depended upon forever.

For instance, most people think more bad things happen on Monday than on any other day of the week. A simple internet search will quickly reveal a general cynicism about an otherwise innocent day. Here are just a few:

*Step Aside Monday . . . This is a job for Coffee!*[38]
*Keep Calm and Pretend it's not Monday.* [39]
*If Monday had a face, I would punch it.* [40]

Imagine the following scenario took place on a Monday. Your alarm clock quit working so you are going to be late for work. Your dog decided it was good time to chew up the edge of your couch. Your coffeemaker, which was working fine yesterday, suddenly won't turn on. It rained overnight exposing a leak in the roof. Fortunately, the leak is in the garage but the water is dripping on your car which has a dead battery and won't start.

It would be easy to conclude this is the result of some Monday curse that created a chain reaction of trouble. The same scenario could just as easily have happened on a Wednesday. It was also just as likely each of these events could have emerged on separate days. Nevertheless, we like to hold to the idea that Monday possesses a special magnet for trouble.

Our independence also leads us to repeat the same patterns over and over, whether it is logical to do so or not. We developed these patterns because they worked for us in the past. Having experienced success, we convince ourselves we can prosper again if we just follow the same pattern. What we refer to as a pattern may not be a pattern at all. It may be the result of a series of random processes but we convince ourselves it is a pattern we can trust.

One of the clearest examples can be found among die hard sports fans. There is widespread belief that my team will play better if I follow a consistent routine on game day. Clay Davis, reporting for Fox Sports, cites a few fascinating examples:

Ellen Irvine is a committed University of Alabama

fan who hangs a ratty old banner on her porch every game. She reports, "I have newer things I put out also, but I always take them down and hang up the old faded banner before game time."

Stannon Banks, takes credit for much of the team's success. "Starting with the 2009 season, I have to be eating a grilled Conecah (smoked sausage sandwich) with honey during the kickoff of the first Bama game of the season. I'm batting .666. Not too bad."

Auburn graduate Terrell Stoves said that he MUST wear his AU shirt to work the day before any big game. "When I don't, we lose to Clemson . . ."

Preston Jones refused to wash the jersey he wears for every game even though he admits it smelled like dirty gym socks by the end of this season.

Clay himself admits to his own dependence upon a Lucky Shirt. The Lucky Shirt system works as follows: If my team wins, I must wear the shirt I have on for every game day until they lose. If the team loses, I cannot simply wash the shirt and try again the next week. Oh no. The tarnished clothing must be retired and a brand-new, never-lost, ultimate winning shirt must be bought . . . As fans, we truly believe what we are doing helps push our team to victory.[41]

We all know these patterns don't really affect the outcome of the game but we engage in them anyway and like to believe that in some mysterious way we helped the team. We incorporate these behaviors into our lives because our brains love to see patterns. Bruce Poulsen, Ph.D. states, "Our brains are pattern-detection machines that connect the dots, making it possible to uncover meaningful relationships among the barrage of sensory input we face."[42] Despite the tendency to see patterns where none exist, this is a valuable characteristic because life is filled with patterns. It is necessary to both our survival and success to recognize them. Identifying dangerous driving conditions, for example, from adverse weather conditions is vital. An early diagnosis of a serious illness based on the pattern of symptoms you observe may be the difference between life and death.

It is wise to train yourself to see patterns. It is just as wise to ask if the patterns you see are based on reality or independent overconfidence.

**Networks**

The universal desire of mankind is to be connected with others. As a result, we all look for a group to belong to. It may be a formal group such as a community organization, religious congregation or professional association. Or, it may be an informal association such as a friendship circle. When it comes to investing, most people feel better about their decisions if they know others are doing the same thing. If a large group is investing in certain stocks, for example, others will conclude there must be something they don't know about and will join the movement.

We all know that "everybody else is doing it" is not a logical reason to do anything but we do it anyway. If you are a parent, you can hear your own voice echoing in your mind, "If everyone else jumped off a cliff, would you jump off a cliff also." The answer, of course, is "No, I wouldn't," and yet you know your own tendency to be blinded by the crowd so it doesn't look like a cliff!

One of the clearest examples in our times is the Ponzi scheme put together by the "esteemed financial expert" Bernie Madoff. He built a solid reputation by helping to found the NASDAQ stock exchange. Alongside the scheme, he operated a legitimate business that made it possible for him to get funds to his investors when they requested withdrawals. Over two decades of operation, thousands of people got caught up in the investment. The interesting thing about the scheme is that it was never actually discovered. In 2008, Madoff himself "revealed that the asset management arm of his firm, Bernard L. Madoff Investment Securities, was 'just one big lie.'" The SEC never sensed a need to investigate thoroughly because thousands of investors were engaged with the company and none of them were complaining. As more people got involved, more people got involved. When all was said and done, "it's estimated he took his investors for a cool $65 billion."

In 2009, Madoff pleaded guilty and was sentenced to 150 years in prison.[43] Unfortunately, the power of the herd stampeded many innocent people's life savings.

There is certainly nothing wrong with moving together with a network of people. In fact, there is power in cooperation that is not attainable as an individual. This is one of the reasons smart investors seek out financial professionals who can advise them and help them discover how other successful individuals are investing their money.  The key is to choose a network that is heading in a healthy direction before you begin to follow.

### Doubts

The feelings of pain we experience when we lose something is a significant force in our lives. In fact, it is stronger than the joy people feel when they gain a comparable amount. In an overly simplified example, if you found a $100 bill on the ground you would feel a certain level of joy. If you then lost that same $100 dollar bill, you would feel an even greater level of pain. At the end of the day, you would have the same amount of money you started with but you would feel worse! The same dollar amount creates different levels of emotional response.

To avoid the pain that may come because of a perceived loss, people will doubt their ability to figure out complex decisions and will hesitate to take risks they would otherwise consider appropriate. We have probably all known a young person who is "deeply in love" with someone that everyone else thinks is a poor choice. We say things to this loved one such as:

"This young man is going to take you away from the people who care about you the most."

"This young lady is manipulating you and you are losing your identity."

"This person is ruining your morals."

"You are giving up everything you used to say is important to you."

"If you marry this person, you are going to have a hard life."

Much to our chagrin, these appeals fall on deaf ears. This young person perceives the relationship is adding value to his or her life and doubts that anyone else could bring this same feeling. To lose that perceived value is more painful than any criticism he or she may have to confront from others. They respond with comments such as:

"Nobody has ever loved me like this."

"He treats me better than anyone I have ever known."

"She makes me a better person."

"She believes in me."

"He accepts me for who I am."

In these cases, the perceived gains outweigh the potential losses and create a magnetic bond between the two.

This creates some fascinating tendencies among the average investor. Some people will hold onto investments longer than they should in hopes the security will rebound rather than admit they have to take a loss. Some will also avoid wise long-term investments because they are afraid they will lose money in the short run. Another trend is for people to sell off investments when they drop in value even if there is historical evidence to believe that ten years from now this will be an attractive part of the portfolio.

As you consider your investment strategy for the future, you will need to look for a balance of losses and gains that you are comfortable with. More conservative investments will offer modest gains with very little risk. Aggressive investments will probably result in higher gains over time but will be characterized by seasons of gain followed by seasons of loss. If you track these more aggressive investments closely, you will have seasons of joy followed by seasons of pain and only you can judge if this is acceptable to you.

## Speculation

Most people speculate in a couple of ways. First, we like to believe that gambling might just pay off. This is not to say that most people are reckless, habitual gamblers who tend to make chaotic financial decisions. The fact that you are reading this book probably means you are more level headed and conservative than that. There is, however, a secret place in our hearts that likes to believe we can win the lottery. The mysterious notion that we can spend just a little bit of money and reap wildly exorbitant returns lurks in our souls and will activate when we think the atmosphere is right.

The other way people speculate is believing that random processes can produce predictable outcomes. Ask the average person, "If a slot machine has not paid out in a while, do you believe it is more likely or less likely to hit the jackpot soon?" Most people will express the belief that slot machines are programmed to pay out on a regular basis to keep people interested. In reality, they are programmed to operate randomly based on probability algorithms. Each "pull of the lever" has the same probability of paying out as the previous pull.

In a less emotional scenario, ask the average citizen, "If I have flipped a quarter 7 times and it landed with the heads up every time, do you think the next toss is more likely or less likely to be heads?" The average person will probably say it is less likely because it has already happened 7 times in a row. In reality, the chances of heads showing is 50% just like every toss before.

These are harmless examples of how people hold onto hope despite the facts. When it comes to simple games, it can be a lot of fun. When it comes to retirement planning, it can be devastating.

## Do I Move or Collect?

Janet never thought about what type of investor style she possessed. She simply thought of retirement planning as a generic activity that everyone pursued in the same way. It seemed confusing and complicated to her so she just trusted that her company's plan for creating a 401(k) plan was the best course of action. In her late fifties, she was unexpectedly called into a meeting with life changing implications. "We are moving your job to a new city. You can move with the company and retain your current position or you can accept a lump sum early retirement agreement." Her plan had been to work until 65 and, based on the information she received at work, she believed she would have enough money to retire at that point. These new options changed all that.

Her entire family lived in the town where she worked so the thought of moving to a new city was not very attractive. She wanted to stay close to her family so she accepted the early retirement, even though she had no idea how to determine if the amount was sufficient to support her. On a whim, she went to her bank to seek advice without asking any strategic questions about her preferred approach to investing or the qualifications of the associate assigned to her case. The associate was inexperienced and limited in his understanding of investment options. He seemed like a nice man, though, so she followed his direction and put her retirement funds in an IRA.

This would have been fine if she was planning to work for another 10 years but her goal was to try to live off her retirement funds, spend more time with her kids and grandkids and get involved in community activities she had put off for the sake of her career. She soon found out that taking withdrawals from an IRA incur a 10% penalty. In addition, it was late in 2008 and the stock market turned volatile. In the first few weeks, her IRA lost 5% of its value! Well, the pain of losing this hard earned money got her attention and she sought help.

We helped her see that there were other options for her retirement funds than an IRA and we helped her set up a way to receive a monthly income without incurring the usual 10% fee. She then determined to get more educated about how investments work and what her options were. In the process, she discovered that she is a Collector. She likes to have a variety of investments in her fund ranging from very safe to moderately risky. She likes the security of predictable approaches but she likes a little thrill from seeing if a more aggressive strategy will pay off. She took a keen interest in the progress of her account and began reviewing her investments quarterly. When she deemed it appropriate, she would make changes. Since 2009, she has averaged a little over 8% return on her investments and has been able to accomplish the goals that were in her heart. She still battles the urge to believe her funds will take care of themselves without oversight but she is getting more comfortable every year being a Collector who balances a variety of investments into a winning combination.

*Chapter 12*

# CHANGING HOW THE WIND BLOWS

The W.I.N.D.S. of financial decisions affect us because they have a place in our hearts. Since their influence lies within, we can change them if we choose. You may be very pleased with the combination of your basic investing style and the way it adjusts to the winds of life. In that case, be grateful and keep doing what you are doing. If, however, you are unhappy with your current outcomes or you sense something is off balance in your financial planning, wisdom says something ought to change.

It's simple to say, "Choose to do things differently." If it were that easy, there would be no need for books, seminars, consultants, or discussions over coffee. The challenge exists because your financial strategies are locked in your heart. You have both intellectual and emotional "reasons" for how you handle money and they both need to be adjusted if you are going to make real changes that stick.  If you are interested in making this kind of adjustment in your life, you can make it happen one step at a time.

**Step 1:** Gather new information.

Exposing yourself to new facts and ways of thinking won't automatically change the way you behave but all effective change begins in the mind. Read books from others who are skilled at what you would like to learn. Attend seminars from experts in the field. Ask others in your social circle who have experienced the type of success you are seeking. Write down the principles you find most helpful and review them until they become second nature to you (most people find this takes between 7 and 21 times).

The *Change Starts with Me* leadership campaign is a good example. Part of the program is a commitment by participants to develop agreed upon character traits. One of the traits is respect. It would be easy to assume everyone knows what this means but various people will have various definitions. The program, therefore, takes time to define the term. Respect means:

- Showing high regard for authority, other people, self and country.
- Treating others as you would want to be treated. To understand that all people have value.
- Listening without interrupting.

As you read this definition, you are challenged to compare it to your instincts about respect. Has it occurred to you that listening is part of respect? Would you have included having regard for yourself? Then the program provides a list of 21st Century Skills that would be expressed in someone who has developed respect:

- Critical thinking and problem-solving
- Collaboration across networks and leading by influence
- Effective oral and written communication[44]

This causes you to further evaluate your understanding of respect. Am I a critical thinker? Do I solve problems effectively? Am I able to collaborate and lead with influence? How are my communication skills?

This information is useful to begin the process of change but knowing these things is not enough to actually create change. Possessing the knowledge that respect will motivate you to become a valuable problem-solver doesn't guarantee you have the necessary skills.

**Step 2:** Make deliberate choices based on this new information.

Say you set a goal to become a more skilled problem-solver. To take it from information to a skill, you will need to put yourself in situations that require problem-solving. In other words, you will have to volunteer to face problems! Once you get in these situations, you can apply what you know about solving problems to test your abilities. This "real world' experience reveals how well your skills are operating and where you need to improve. Each adjustment helps transform your knowledge into a skill.

**Step 3:** Push past the fear barrier.

Anytime you make fundamental changes in the way you think, act or feel you will encounter fear. Fear sets up roadblocks in front of the way you want to go in an attempt to stop any real change. You can't reason with it or go around it. You have to knock down the roadblock to stay on the path.

In our example of becoming a skilled problem-solver, you will probably be hesitant to insert yourself into known problems. You may be afraid of inadequacy or feeling overwhelmed. There is, however, no substitute for active engagement. To develop the skill, you have to push past the fear of facing problems and face them anyway. Each success you experience will hone the skill and raise your confidence.

Steve Goodier recounts the story of how Henry Ward Beecher, the famed 19th century clergyman, social reformer, and abolitionist pushed past the fear barrier in his life.

When Beecher was a young boy in school, he was called upon to recite in front of the class. He had hardly begun when the teacher interrupted with an emphatic, "No!" He started over and again the teacher thundered, "No!" Humiliated, Henry sat down.

The next boy rose to recite and had just begun when the teacher shouted, "No!" This student, however, kept on with the recitation until he completed it. As he sat down, the teacher replied, "Very good!"

Henry was irritated. "I recited just as he did," he complained to the teacher.

But the instructor replied, "It is not enough to know your lesson, you must be sure. When you allowed me to stop you, it meant that you were uncertain. If the world says, 'No!' it is your business to say, 'Yes!' and prove it.

The world will say, 'No!' in a thousand ways.

'No! You can't do that.'

'No! You are wrong.'

'No! You are too old.'

'No! You are too young.'

'No! You are too weak.'

'No! It will never work.'

'No! You don't have the education.'

'No! You don't have the background.'

'No! You don't have the money.'

'No! It can't be done.'

And each 'No!' you hear has the potential to erode your confidence bit by bit until you quit all together. Though the world says, 'No!' to you today, you should be determined to say, 'Yes!' and prove it!"[45]


**Step 4:** Gather a team of supporters.

Real change is hard on us because it disconnects us from the habits we are used to in hopes of discovering a better way of doing life. It is similar to traveling from one land to another on a high bridge. When you start out, it is fun and exciting. You are motivated to leave unproductive habits behind and are excited about a new way of life. Halfway across the bridge, the fog rolls in and the wind begins to blow. It is easy to feel lost and alone. Other travelers who are cheering you on are strong motivators to finish the journey. When a farmer has a minor fence repair, he will simply take care of it himself. If there is major damage, he will likely call his friends to assist since many hands make light work. If you are all alone, it is predictable that you will turn back to the habits you are used to. Your support team could be friends who are seeking the same kind of change, advisors who are coaching you to victory or professional associates who are serving as mentors.

**Step 5:** Celebrate every victory!

You are seeking to rewire your emotional connection to life's decisions. Emotions don't normally respond to logic but they do respond to compliments, criticism and cheers. You are probably going to make some mistakes along the way and it will be easy to be critical and condemning of yourself. If you dwell there, you may undermine the very change you are hoping to make. You are also going to make some great decisions and reach some very solid conclusions. If you reward yourself, regardless of how big or small the victory may be, your heart begins to be reprogrammed to expect good results.

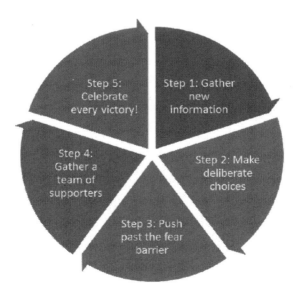

As you train yourself to think and act in a different way, you will grow in wisdom. You may even surprise yourself with brilliant solutions to complex decisions, as Sridhar Krishnan reports in the following account:

Many years ago in a small Zezuru village, a farmer had the misfortune of owing a large sum of money to a village moneylender. The moneylender, who was old and ugly, fancied the farmer's young, beautiful daughter. So the moneylender proposed a bargain. He said he would forgo the farmer's debt if he could marry his daughter. Both the farmer and his daughter were horrified by the proposal.

So the cunning money-lender suggested that they let providence decide the matter. He told them that he would put a black pebble and a white pebble into an empty money bag. Then the girl would have to pick one pebble from the bag. If she picked the black pebble, she would become his wife and her father's debt would be forgiven. If she picked the white pebble she need not marry him and her father's debt would still be forgiven. But if she refused to pick a pebble, her father would be thrown into jail.

As they talked, the moneylender bent over to pick up two pebbles. As he picked them up, the sharp-eyed girl noticed that he had picked up two black pebbles and put them into the bag. He then asked the girl to pick a pebble from the bag.

The quick thinking girl put her hand into the moneybag and drew out a pebble. Without looking at it, she fumbled and let it fall onto the pebble-strewn path where it immediately became lost among all the other pebbles.

"Oh, how clumsy of me," she said. "But never mind, if you look into the bag for the one that is left, you will be able to tell which pebble I picked." Since the remaining pebble is black, it must be assumed that she had picked the white one. And since the money-lender dared not admit his dishonesty, the girl changed what seemed an impossible situation into an extremely advantageous one.[46]

People may tell you that change is impossible. You may even feel in your heart the change you desire is too difficult. You will never know until you try and the journey begins with a single step.

# Section 5

## HEALTHCARE

*Chapter 13*

# A PLAN THAT MATCHES YOU

Americans are retiring in record numbers as approximately 8,000 Americans turn 65 each day.[47] When it is your turn, you enter retirement with anticipation. You've worked hard building your career. You've adjusted through the ups and downs of life. You've maintained your health sufficiently so that you could decide to retire. It is now time to enjoy the benefits of the sacrifices you have made.

It doesn't happen automatically, however. It takes planning and preparation to fund the facets of your life that accompany your retirement years. One of the most misunderstood areas is healthcare. Because the average person doesn't understand the demands and nuances of healthcare coverage, it is also one of the most neglected. Despite the challenges and confusion that can arise, none of us can afford to ignore this need.

## It's in the Savings

The Employee Benefit Research Institute (EBRI) released a study in October 2014 addressing how much the average retiree needs to save to cover anticipated health care costs during retirement. Their results are based on a number of assumptions which include:

- Your retirement budget includes expenses for two people.
- You have traditional Medicare insurance.
- Your prescription medication use is in the 90th percentile of all Americans.

Based on these assumptions, the EBRI estimates that the

average couple will need in excess of $300,000 in savings to cover their health care costs.[48] It appears that most people either don't know about these estimates or don't believe they are reliable since "a recent poll of pre-retirees (ages 55-64) found that nearly half (48 percent) of respondents believe they will only need $50,000 to pay for health care costs in retirement."[49]

Results like these lead me to conclude that healthcare costs in retirement are widely misunderstood.

Since it can be overwhelming to view healthcare costs as a lump sum, it may help if we take a look at the costs on an annual basis. "According to an analysis by the Kaiser Family Foundation (KFF), health expenses accounted for 14% of Medicare household budgets in 2012, or $4,792 per year."[50] This means the average couple can anticipate paying about $5,000 per year on health care if they have Medicare as their primary insurance. You have options, of course, in the way you address these costs. You may cover these costs through traditional savings, a health savings account, your operating budget, or a combination of these approaches. You probably don't have the choice to just ignore the issue hoping you won't have serious healthcare issues but you do have options in how you meet the need.

### It Pays to Get Covered

Retirement is a great time of life. You have worked hard and you ought to enjoy years of doing what you would like and seeing the people you want to see. Worrying about potential healthcare costs will add stress to your life and steal energy. To help alleviate this stress, you will want to secure some kind of medical insurance to insure that most of your medical costs will be covered. Your primary options include:

- Employer based coverage that is part of your pension package.
- Medicare

- A policy provided by a private company.

I am consistently amazed at the responses I receive when I ask people why they chose their current medical coverage. The most common responses I get are:

> "When I retired, I asked my good friend, Paul. He suggested I go with company X. He said their insurance worked for him."

> "I lost my coverage and I had to do something. I went to a seminar where they told me this policy was equivalent to what I had before."

> "I didn't have much to spend on health insurance but I knew I needed coverage. I chose this one because I could afford it."

Regardless of the reasons, almost no one I meet truly understands how their coverage works. Few understand the balance between the cost of their premiums and the amount they must pay out of their pocket. Even fewer are familiar with the limits of the policies or the exceptions they will undoubtedly face in the future. They simply knew they needed something or they could find themselves in a bad situation.

### The Affordable Care Act

The Affordable Care Act (popularly known as Obamacare) has made healthcare more accessible to those with preexisting conditions which has been good news to many who were previously unable to secure coverage. The ACA has also helped many with low incomes secure much needed coverage. It has, at the same time, devastated the checkbooks and budgets of many in the middle class. The combination of high and escalating rates has made it difficult for many who are responsible for providing their own healthcare.

### Ask Questions

The way health care insurance is sold today has created an overwhelming amount of creative coverage options. It is impossible for any one person to be familiar with all of them or to even be up to date on the latest innovations in health care coverage. As a result, the best thing you can do is ask questions about the policies available to you until you are confident one meets your needs at an acceptable level. Your first question is probably, "What questions should I ask? What are the facts and circumstances that will impact my choices?" Your situation is unique to you so there are likely going to be individualized questions you will need to pursue. There are, however, a few basic questions that all of us ought to consider that create a great starting point for your conversation with your health care coverage professional.

*How much is the premium?* This is the starting point in your financial discussions about health insurance. No policy is generally free so there will be some kind of monthly fee that must be paid in order to keep your policy in force.

*Does this policy involve copayments?* It is common for modern medical policies to include copayments, though there are some that don't. This is money you pay directly to the doctor, hospital or pharmacy for services or products. It is generally a small percentage of the overall cost but it will come out of your personal budget.

*How much are the deductibles and what is the maximum out of pocket costs in this policy?* Most policies include a maximum amount that you as the policyholder will be required to pay during the calendar year. If you choose a higher deductible and out of pocket limit, the monthly premium you pay will be lower. If you opt for a lower deductible and out of pocket agreement, you will need to pay more per month for your coverage.

*Which doctors and hospitals can I utilize with this coverage?* Some policies allow you to choose the doctor and hospital you will use. Others have approved physicians and facilities that must be used in order for the insurance to cover the bills. Since health care involves an important relationship between you and your doctors, it is important to know if the professionals you want to utilize are included in your coverage.

*Are there major exceptions in this policy I should be aware of?* No insurance company has unlimited resources so they must make decisions in the coverage limits they offer. Many companies offer standard policies for the most common health issues faced by their clients. To keep monthly prices down, they will include exceptions for the more unusual or drastic health challenges. They may exclude certain coverages or increase the deductible a patient is required to pay for certain ailments. Before you purchase a policy, you will want to know what these exceptions are.

### Run it through your grid

The answers to these questions will give you information you can compare with your personal grid. The grid you use to help you make health care decisions is very personal to you and can be discovered by working through another set of questions:

*How much risk are you comfortable with?* Some of you reading this are quite comfortable with risk. You are confident in your ability to save and invest money. If a catastrophic medical event interrupted your life, you honestly believe you will have put enough money aside to address it. Others of you are frightened by the thought. Whatever policy you choose ought to be in line with the level of risk you prefer.

*How much coverage do you prefer to carry?* We are privileged in the sense that we have many options available to us. You can, if you prefer, purchase a policy with small copayments and a small deductible. This type will be more expensive per month but will require you to spend little out of pocket when you need health care. On the other hand, you can purchase a policy with a high deductible and more aggressive copayments. This will cost you less per month and, if you remain healthy, will cost you little out of pocket.

*How important is it for you to choose your doctor?* Some policies require you to use doctors, hospitals and specialists who are part of their network. Going outside the network can result in higher costs to you or in the company denying coverage. Other policies give you the freedom to choose the doctors and hospital you prefer.

*How much do you plan to travel during retirement?* Some policies will provide coverage no matter where you are or which medical facility you visit. Others will limit your options or require you to identify services ahead of time in the area you are traveling.

Each option has benefits and liabilities. Each option will provide certain services you highly value and withhold certain benefits you would prefer to have. There is no perfect policy but intelligent conversations with a competent adviser can help you identify the coverage that best fits your situation.

# Section 5

---

# LIFE INSURANCE

# Chapter 14

# LIFE INSURANCE IS LIKE A TRACTOR

Having a life insurance policy is a lot like owning a Tractor. At its core, a tractor is a vehicle with a strong engine and good traction that is used for pushing, pulling or towing objects that would otherwise be hard to move. The word tractor originated from the Latin word "trahere," which means "to pull." When tractors were first created, they were simple vehicles with limited capabilities. They were originally designed to replace working animals such as oxen and horses. Since pulling things was about the only thing oxen and horses could do, early tractors were designed to pull. In fact, part of Henry Ford's inspiration for the automobile came from a sincere desire to find a better way to do heavy farm work.

> "I felt perfectly certain that horses, considering all the bother of attending them and the expense of feeding, did not earn their keep. The obvious thing to do was to design and build a steam engine that would be light enough to run an ordinary wagon or to pull a plow. I thought it more important first to develop the tractor. To lift farm drudgery off flesh and blood and lay it on steel and motors has been my most constant ambition."[51]

Through the innovation of farmers and the advancement of modern technology, tractors have now become incredibly versatile.[52] Today, tractors can be found in various types and sizes and can address almost any function you can imagine on the farm or around the yard.

The basic tractor is arguably the most important piece of machinery on the farm. It has been described as:

- "The lifeblood of the farm."[53]
- "Our mechanical beast."[54]
- "Truly amazing vehicles."[55]
- "It's a tool that I must use to keep Mother Nature at bay."[56]
- "A farm boy remembers the first car he drove, the first girl he kissed and the first tractor he drove."[57]

## My First Tractor

Having grown up as a "country boy," I can say with certainty that I will never forget my first. Dad had an old Allis Chalmers tractor. I was just 12 years-old but I thought I was much older when he told me I could take it by myself to the neighbor's pigpen. I had just gotten my hunting license and my dad let me work for the local farmers so I could afford to hunt. The tractor was already on the dirt road facing the neighbor's property. I jumped up and started it with great enthusiasm. I slipped it into gear and started down the road. I plotted the course in my mind from our house to the pigpen. I steered right when it was time to steer right. I steered left when it was time to steer left. With remarkable skill, I arrived at the neighbor's plot of land just in time to feed the pigs. After doing my chores, I started up the tractor once again and retraced my path back home. It was one of the greatest achievements of my young life.

What I didn't realize was the foolproof nature of the farmer's plan. From our house to the neighbor's, the dirt road was fitted with massive ruts. The tires of the tractor slipped into the ruts and would only exit with focused adult skill and strength. I thought I was steering the tractor that had no choice but to follow the path prescribed by the ruts.

A few years later, my dad let me have a "real" turn driving his tractor. It was May. We had been hired to plow a field that was 8 or 9 miles away. We connected the plow to the three point hitch and raised it up in the air so we could drive to the field. I was sitting on the side of the fender as dad started down the road.

I swelled up with pride like a puffed up rooster getting ready to crow when he turned to me and asked, "Do you want to drive?"

Dad let me drive to the site and lower the plow to the ground. I was completely surprised when my dad took a seat on the fender and told me to drive. I was just a young teenager so I was thrilled. My confidence level soared because I was doing real work and we were going to get paid to do the job!

## Versatile Power

Farm implements can be attached to the rear of the tractor through either a drawbar or a three point hitch. "The three-point hitch was invented by Harry Ferguson and has been standard since the 1960s."[58] In addition, many tractors have a Power Take Off (PTO) with a shaft that rotates which can operate additional equipment such as snow blowers, grass mowers, rotary brooms, etc.

People will buy a tractor because they need to pull or push something but soon realize it is capable of much more if the need arises. In the same way, people buy life insurance because they want to provide the security of a death benefit for the people they love but they soon realize it is capable of meeting a number of other needs over the life of the policy.

There is a wide variety of equipment that can be attached to a tractor to meet the needs and desires of just about any customer. In addition to being a pulling vehicle, a tractor can be any or all of the following tools:

- A bulldozer with a large dozing blade for moving large amounts of dirt.
- A backhoe with a large digging bucket that can

create ditches in record time.

- A front loader with a bucket that can scoop, smooth and transport.
- A disk that will break up ground.
- A section harrow which will till the ground and arrange it in rows for planting.
- A middle buster which will dig a trench in the middle of a row to lay down seeds.
- A hay cutter for cutting hay (just to state the obvious).
- A hay rake to move the hay into even rows after it has cured in the sun.
- A hay baler that gathers up the rows of hay, spins them into bales, ties them up and drops them on the field to be picked up later.
- A sprayer for applying weed control or fertilizer.
- A posthole digger for setting fence posts (When you don't have young boys who need to be trained to value hard work).
- A mower that can cut large yards or expansive fields.
- A snow blower for clearing walkways, driveways and private roadways during the winter months.
- A hay wagon for transporting bales of hay or giving hay rides at a community celebration!

And this is just the tip of the iceberg on all the things that a tractor can accomplish for the creative and motivated user.

## More Work, Less Effort

Curtis Von Fange illustrates the versatility of his family's tractor in an article entitled, Tractor Implements, which he wrote as a tribute to his dad.

Dad was raised during the depression years of the thirties. As a kid he worked part time on a farm in Kansas doing many of the manual chores. My dad dreamed that some day he would have his own tractor with every implement he could get. When he reached his early sixties, he got his dream.

Probably the most universal implement that came with dad's tractor was the front end loader. In the winter he would clean the snow off the driveway and make huge hills that the kids would play on for days. In the summer it was used for work projects such as digging out sections of dirt for extending the driveway or making a place for some fuel oil barrels. The bucket was great for carrying tools around the property, trash to the street, or taking grandkids for a ride to the mailbox.

It seems like the grass never stops growing in the spring. Dad could usually keep up with it, though, by using his Bush Hog®. It's amazing what this five foot diameter unit can do when it is properly matched to the tractor size, weight, and horsepower.

I think it was mom who wanted the garden, but dad got to prepare it. Fortunately, his plow and disc made the job more enjoyable. The plow was a single bottom with a three point hitch.

Fixing fences was always a chore in the old days, but at least our tractor could take much of the work away. Dad's post hole digger would reduce pole setting time down to a minimum. We would go through the field and auger out the holes. Then we would hook up the wagon, load it with fence posts, and drive along the fence row while someone dropped the posts in each hole. All that was left was for us "kids" to tamp down the dirt so the posts would stand straight.

As time went on, dad kept increasing his inventory so he wouldn't have to do much of the hard physical labor he remembered as a young man.[59]

## The Primary Reason: You are Valuable

Why do people buy life insurance? Just like a tractor, there is a primary reason people acquire coverage even though they realize there's a number of benefits to be enjoyed from their purchase.

The most common reason you may consider purchasing life insurance is the value of your life. The money you earn provides housing, food, transportation, education, vacations and shared memories for you and your family. In other words, your income provides both tangible (ways you can measure) and intangible (ways you can feel but may not be able to quantify) value to your life and relationships. You have grown to depend on this source of income. You make plans based on what you expect to earn. You compile budgets based on your salary. And, you dream of great moments you can create with those you love.

Then, in the back of your mind, a thought looms that you can't ignore but would rather not think about - I may not live as long as I have planned. None of us likes to think about death and we certainly would never allow the thought of our demise to be the driving force behind our goals. If something did happen, however, we would put the people we love in a bad situation. They would suddenly realize how valuable we are in terms of providing financial and emotional support. There is no straightforward way to replace the emotional strength you invest in your loved ones but there is a simple, dependable way to replace the income from which they otherwise would have benefited. As a result, the primary function of a life insurance policy is to create an immediate estate for your family.

Since life insurance is an emotional gift of love based on the eventual truth that we will all pass from this earth, people can be funny when it comes to insurance. The average person doesn't hesitate when it comes to insuring their homes, their cars and their health. When it comes to life insurance, however, it is a different story which can lead to some absurd conversations. For instance:

One agent took advantage of the emotional nature of life

insurance when he said to his client, "Don't let me frighten you into a hasty decision. Sleep on it tonight. If you wake in the morning, give me a call then and let me know."[60]

Another lady who didn't like to think about life insurance wrote her insurance company a letter asking to cancel her husband's life insurance policy. "We've always paid on time" she explained, "but since my dear husband passed away, I have some financial difficulties and can no longer afford to pay you the yearly premium!"[61]

A third lady who recognized the value of her husband's policy had the following conversation with her son:

"Mom, I want to go swimming into the sea"

The mother replied, "No son, the weather is not good, the sea is rough and it is pretty unsafe and risky. Slight carelessness could lead to fatal injuries."

"But Mom, why didn't you stop Dad from swimming in the sea?"

"Don't worry, son, his life is insured"[62]

The bottom line is that you matter and you will be missed. One of the great gifts of love you can give to the people you care about is life insurance coverage that will help them adjust. An experienced, dependable professional can help you determine the amount of life insurance that will provide your family the level of income you want them to have. You may determine you have enough with your employer supplied policy or you may decide that more is in order.

### It is a Gift of Love
In addition to providing a financial safety net for your family, a life insurance policy can cover the impact of funeral

costs and mortuary services. If your loved ones lose you, they will be thrust into the grieving process. They will be flooded with emotions that surprise them. They will feel extremely sad at times. They will feel apathetic and listless at times. At other times they will simply be angry. Then, in a moment of relief, they will hear themselves laughing only to feel guilty about having a good time this close to your death. It is a highly charged emotional roller coaster that no one can rescue them from. In the midst of this roller coaster, they are supposed to make strategic financial decisions about your funeral. If you have taken time to preplan and if you have life insurance that will pay the bills of those plans, your family members will be given a much needed break. They will be confident because they know they are carrying out your plans. They will also be more relaxed because they don't have to worry about where the money is coming from.

**The Mysterious Value**

It helps us understand the value of life insurance when we accept that the term "life insurance" is one of life's profound mysteries. We call it "life" insurance but your beneficiaries only benefit from it when you are no longer alive. This idea reminds me of some of my favorite quotes and questions about life's mysteries:

*"I have never let my schooling interfere with my education." – Mark Twain* [63]

*"If there is a 50-50 chance that something can go wrong, then nine times out of ten it will." – Paul Harvey* [64]

*"It requires a very unusual mind to undertake the analysis of the obvious." – Alfred North Whitehead* [65]

*Why is the third hand on the watch called the second hand?*

*Why does "fat chance" and "slim chance" mean the same thing?*

*Why are a "wise man" and a "wise guy" opposites?*

*Why do we drive on a parkway and park on a driveway?* [66]

## The Tractor Effect

Covering your value to your family and the costs of your funeral are like the engine on a tractor. Your policy, however, may be able to do a lot more which makes life insurance a valuable part of your future financial planning. Some of the possibilities include:

*Mortgage Protection.* You may not be the only source of income in your family but you are certainly a significant financial contributor. Your spouse may work. You may have investments or proceeds from a family business that help with your monthly expenses. If something were to happen to you, therefore, your family would not lose all their income stream. In this case, you may want life insurance to take the burden of a mortgage off your family members. Even though they still have an income, it certainly is not as much as it used to be and the security of knowing they can stay in their home will help them make the transition to the new season of their life easier.

*Transfer wealth to your family.* One of the great motivators of life is taking care of your family. Every parent wants his/her kids to have a better life than they had. Every grandparent wants their grandkids to be healthy and financially stable. This is one of the reasons we work so hard and build solid careers. The last thing we want at the end of our lives is to give most of our money to the government. We want our kids and grandkids to benefit from the income we worked so hard to establish. Life insurance is one way to insure that much of your estate ends up in the hands of your loved ones.

*Cash Value with Tax Advantages.* Some life insurance policies create cash value as you pay your premiums. Although the payments are not tax deductible, the earnings are not taxed as income while they are accumulating. Life insurance can, therefore, be a strategic element in building wealth for your future.

*Keeping Up with College.* It is a ridiculous understatement to say that college is expensive. Yearly tuition, housing, living expenses, books and supplies add up to thousands of dollars per year. The evidence that a college education has become a daunting venture is the number of people currently paying on college loans. According to American Student Assistance, "Nearly 20 million Americans attend college each year and close to 12 million (60%) borrow money annually to help cover the costs." As a result, more than 40 million Americans are carrying a student loan with an average outstanding balance of $24,300.[67]   The average rate is growing too as student loan balances for current graduates has risen to more than $30,000.[68]  To put it in perspective, the 40 million Americans with student loan debt represents more people than live in many countries including Canada, Poland, North Korea or Australia.[69]

This trend is not likely to end any time soon. It is still recognized that a college degree usually results in greater earning potential. Many families like the prestige and sense of accomplishment that accompanies a college degree so they encourage their kids to do whatever it takes to pursue an education. Also, the federal government is making a lot of money off student loans. Kyle McCarthy, co-founder of StudentDebtCrisis.org commented in the Huffington Post, "The Congressional Budget Office projects that the Federal Government made about $50 billion on student loans in 2013. This is $5 billion more than ExxonMobile, the most profitable company in the country."[70]

While you are working and making a sufficient salary, student loans can be incorporated into your budget. If you pass away, the burden lands on your family. Life insurance can be a safeguard to make sure student loans are paid in the case of an unforeseen accident or illness.

## To Catch a Thief

It seems the innovation of mankind knows no limits so it is probably no surprise that tractors have been used for some surprising ventures. The story of Zanescot Kester is one such example. He runs Zanescot Kester Lawn and Tree service in Valles Mines, Missouri, which is about 50 miles south of St. Louis. As part of his business, he sells a lot of firewood. On May 21, 2015, he was back in the woods on an unmarked gravel road cutting and collecting wood. He was using his tractor to transport loads of firewood to his dump truck. At 1:40 in the afternoon, he saw his truck driving away.

"As I was coming out of the woods I saw my truck and trailer leaving — we're talking a ½ mile back in the woods!" Kester said.

"I just put it high gear and went after him!" he said.

Kester called the Sheriff's Department as he gave chase so he would have some back up help when he confronted the thief. It turned out that the suspect took Kester's truck to try and pull another truck out of the mud. The "other" pickup was stolen also. In trying to free up the first truck from the mud, the robber got Kester's truck stuck also. When Zanecost pulled up on the scene the man was still there and frustrated.

"I brought the tractor right in behind it. I put the bucket down and said, 'bud you ain't going nowhere. The police are on the way. You're just waiting right here.'"

After the man was taken into custody Kester summed up his experience, "I know he stole the wrong one when he stole mine. I would chase him down no matter where he'd go. Nothing runs like a Deere!" he laughed.

Both victims got their trucks back and Zanecost got a story he will tell for the rest of his life.

Tractors and life insurance policies are some of the most versatile tools you will encounter during your journey through life.

# Chapter 15

# SELECTIONS THAT WORK FOR YOU

In lots of ways that people don't normally think about, life insurance adds value to our lives.

Airman Jones was assigned to the induction center where he advised new recruits about their government benefits, especially their GI insurance.

It wasn't long before Captain Smith noticed that Airman Jones had almost a 100% record for insurance sales, which had never happened before. Rather than ask about this, the Captain stood in the back of the room and listened to Jones's sales pitch.

Jones explained the basics of the GI Insurance to the new recruits, and then said: "If you have GI Insurance, go into battle and are killed, the government has to pay $200,000 to your beneficiaries. If you don't have GI insurance, go into battle and get killed, the government only has to pay a maximum of $6000."

"Now," he concluded, "which bunch do you think they are going to send into battle first?"[71]

This doesn't mean, however, that all policies are the same. Just as there are many models of tractors, there are various types of life insurance policies with varying levels of provision and risk.

**Term Insurance**

Term life insurance is the cheapest and simplest life insurance available. In exchange for paying a premium, the life insurance company agrees to pay a certain amount of money to your beneficiaries. Payments are made and the coverage is provided for a designated amount of time (the term). During the entire life of the policy, your payments remain the same. At the end of the term, the policy expires. At that point, you can purchase another policy to take its place or make the decision that the coverage is no longer needed. Because this is a simple policy with a pre-defined period of time, it is the most affordable type of coverage.

There is a variation of the term life insurance policy that has an attractive option to many. It is called the return of premium life insurance. If you are alive at the end of the term of the policy, the insurance company refunds all of your payments. Over time the policy costs you nothing! You, of course, didn't make any money from your premiums but you didn't lose anything either. It will cost more than a pure term policy but if you are in good health and willing to take the risk, it can be a helpful component of your strategy.

**Whole Life Insurance**

Whole life insurance, on the other hand, has no term attached to it. It is designed to cover you for your "whole life." This is a popular cash value type of insurance. That means the policy provides a "death benefit" in the case of your demise but it also has an investment element to it. The company that provides the policy guarantees you will make money on the policy at a certain percentage rate. In addition, if it is held by a mutual company, dividends will be paid on the policy each year based on how well the company performed during the year.

Whole life costs more than term insurance but once you commit to your policy, you will pay the same amount every year. It doesn't cost more as you age and it won't change whether you remain healthy or face health challenges. As long as you keep making payments, your policy is in effect. This is a safe, conservative type of investment because the death benefit is guaranteed, the interest rate at which you will earn money is fixed and the price is guaranteed not to increase.

## Universal Life Insurance

This is similar to whole life in that the company guarantees a minimum annual return. The advantage of this type of policy is in its flexibility. You have the ability to increase or decrease the death benefit and vary premium payments. Some find this attractive because they can easily adjust the policy to match the current experience of their lives. Success with this type of coverage depends upon your ability to dynamically answer the questions:

How much coverage do you need?

How much do you have available in your budget to pay into the policy?

How do you want to space out your payments?

Universal life will cost more than term but less than whole life insurance. It will be attractive to you if you like the flexibility of changing your coverage and your investment in the policy over time. If this type of product interests you, you probably also want to explore cash value universal life options. These policies accumulate value over time as you pay into the policy. When it reaches a certain level, you can borrow money against the the cash value or withdraw money from the policy. If you choose to cancel the policy, the cash value that has accrued in the policy will be returned to you.

## Variable Life Insurance

Variable life policies are similar to whole life in two ways. First, they pay a guaranteed death benefit. Second, the price of the policy never changes so the amount you pay will be the same at age 40, 50, 60 and beyond. The uniqueness of variable life is the choices it gives you to invest the money you have paid in. Some of you have an independent streak in you. You like to be in charge of the details and you like to be in on the decisions. You never want to feel like the man who bemoaned, "Last week I bought a retirement policy. All I have to do is keep up the payments for 15 years and my agent can retire.[72]

You may be a renegade who likes to create your own path or you may be a regulator who has a hard time trusting others with the important decisions of life. Either way, you prefer the process of researching and choosing how your money will be invested. A variable life plan will give you the option to tie your investment to the stock and bond market. If your choices in the market do well, the policy does well. If the market decreases, the policy decreases. If the market is static throughout the year, the policy will show neither an increase nor a decrease. There is more risk in variable life policies with the possibility of earning more cash value than other options. Either way, you have the added benefit of knowing you made the choices.

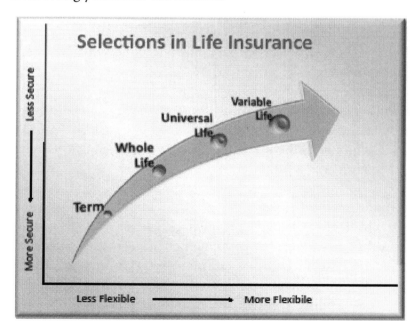

## Life Insurance and the Government

Everybody is motivated by the bottom line and life insurance can help you shelter some of your money from unnecessary taxes. To understand how your life insurance funds will be taxed, it is helpful to break down your life insurance funds into categories.

*The Death Benefit.* All of us at some point have thought to ourselves, I want to leave whatever I can to the people I care about. The list may include your spouse, your kids or grandkids, a favorite charity or close friends. The list has probably never included the government! And yet, the governing officials will sweep in after your demise with estate taxes to take what they consider to be their share of your assets. When you purchase a policy, it has a "face value." This is the amount of money the insurance carrier will pay to your loved ones in the event that your life ends unexpectedly. In almost all cases, this money is completely tax free. For instance, if you have a policy with a benefit of $100,000 your beneficiary will receive the full amount of $100,000 and it will not be included in anyone's taxable income.

*Your Investment.* Over the years, you are going to make payments on your life insurance policy. If it is a cash value policy, you will have the option at some point of withdrawing funds. The amount you paid in over the years can be withdrawn without having to include that amount in your taxable income. If you are fortunate enough to live a long, healthy life, your premiums act like a secure savings account that can be accessed without worrying about the taxes you must pay for putting that money into action.

*Loans from the Policy.* As cash value builds up in your life insurance policy, you are able to take loans from the insurance company based on this amount. The insurer will hold your policy as collateral as they loan you the money at a reasonable rate. Since the money is a loan, it is not a withdrawal from your policy. As a result, it is available tax free to you. Any unpaid balance will be subtracted from any benefits that would be paid out but as you repay the loan, the value of your policy is preserved for future generations. This makes the asset useful now and later without having to worry about imminent tax implications.

## Traditions of Love

Life insurance is a strong statement of your love and concern for your family. When they know you are sacrificing today to make sure they are taken care of tomorrow, their sense of security, importance and confidence can't help but grow. Decisions like these create cherished traditions that cause the family to grow stronger with each generation.

*Chapter 16*

# SURPRISING SOLUTIONS

Nobody knows exactly what life has in store. You may experience a remarkable success that goes "viral" and becomes an unprecedented trend. Or, you may face unexpected financial reversals for which you had no idea you were supposed to prepare. An interesting truth about life insurance shows up in the unfortunate case of a bankruptcy. If your financial situation faces a reversal and you have to apply for bankruptcy, your assets will be scrutinized by creditors. Your life insurance is exempt from this process so any money you have in policies will be sheltered from creditors.

It's also possible you may encounter a great but unexpected opportunity. It may not be absolutely necessary but you or your loved ones may have a strong desire to make it happen. This could include vacations, a once in a lifetime deal on a car, an investment in a new business for one of your relatives, etc. Since certain types of life insurance create cash value that you can borrow against, they have the potential to help fund these opportunities. You didn't set up your life insurance policy for these reasons but, because it is your money, you have control over how you use it. Perhaps you set up a policy to help fund your childs' college education. When your child received a larger scholarship than you anticipated, you didn't end up using it for this purpose. You may decide borrowing money from your policy to celebrate a 25th or 35th anniversary is a good use of the funds. Since the cash value is yours, you have the flexibility to allocate its use however you wish.

The flexibility inherent in life insurance policies has filled the history of the United States with stories of dreams that were partially funded by life insurance loans.

### Disneyland

In 1923, an enterprising young man named Walt Disney opened his studio in Los Angeles, California along with his brother, Roy. One of their early cartoon characters was stolen by a distributor which angered the brothers, as you can imagine. In response, Walt made sure he owned everything he made after that. In 1928, he introduced Mickey Mouse to the world and the energetic mascot became an immediate sensation as the first cartoon to be synchronized with sound. Together Walt, Roy and Mickey revolutionized the world of animation.

By the 1950s, Disney Studios was experiencing steady success through movies and television programming. Being a persistent dreamer, Walt became intrigued with the idea of creating an amusement park where parents and children could have a good time together in a clean, safe environment. Prior to the opening of Disneyland, amusement parks would best be described as run down facilities operated by a less than stellar staff. They were not the kind of places a parent would want to take children and Walt thought this was a shame.

As you can imagine, this type of venture was going to be very pricey. Disney himself said, "It takes a lot of money to make these dreams come true."[73] The project cost about $17 million but the efforts to acquire traditional funding failed. In fact, most people thought the project would be a financial disaster and predicted it would be closed and forgotten within the first year. Even Walt's brother, Roy, thought that a "fanciful, expensive amusement park would lead to financial ruin,"[74] since Walt possessed neither the real estate nor the commercial construction experience to pull off a project of this magnitude.

Walt was not willing to let go of the dream, however, so he looked for other ways to secure the necessary funding. To assemble the initial design team, he sold vacation property and borrowed from his own cash value life insurance. He hadn't purchased his policies for this purpose but when the opportunity presented itself, the assets were in place to help make a dream come true.

It took the help of ABC and a promise by Disney to provide weekly television programming but in 1955 Disneyland opened its gates welcoming more than 3.5 million visitors during its first year. It is still a thriving business today that has created family memories for countless numbers of grandparents, parents and children.

## McDonald's

Another business that has shaped the American landscape is McDonald's. The company was founded by Dick and Mac McDonald in San Bernardino, California. In 1952, the company caught the attention of Ray Kroc who was selling milkshake mixing machines. The success of the brother's hamburger stand made them attractive prospects for Kroc's multimixers which could make multiple shakes all at once. Kroc was fascinated to know how this single hamburger stand in Southern California could use so many milkshake machines so he created time to visit them and study their procedures. While meeting with the McDonald brothers, Kroc discovered they were looking for a nationwide franchising agent. At the age of 52, Ray Kroc concluded there was a bigger future for him in hamburgers than milkshakes so he partnered with Dick and Mac.

He opened his first McDonald's in Des Plaines, Illinois in 1955 with the goal of doing for hamburgers what Henry Ford had done for automobiles. He believed he could set up an efficient "assembly line" that would ensure customers could get the same quality food no matter what McDonalds they visited. Kroc did not take a salary during the first 8 years of his franchising efforts. Think about that. From the age of 52 until he was 60, he took no salary from his company! To overcome the cash flow challenges, he borrowed money from his bank and two cash value life insurance policies he held. These loans helped him keep up with salaries of key employees, vital operating costs and an innovative advertising campaign around an emerging mascot by the name of Ronald McDonald.

Ray Kroc is noted for creating standardization throughout the chain of restaurants so that customers could anticipate the same texture, quality and value whether they were buying burgers in Illinois, Alabama, Minnesota or California. By 1965 (10 years after Ray Kroc opened his first franchise), more than 700 McDonald's restaurants had opened in the United States. By 2012, more than 30,000 McDonalds were open for business serving more than 500 million people each day in 119 countries.

James Cash Penney had it in his heart to be a successful businessman at a young age. In 1898 he went to work at the Golden Rule Store. The owners took notice of his hard work and intrinsic motivation so they offered him a 1/3 partnership in a new store they were opening in Kemmerer, Wyoming. The store grew and Penney participated in opening two more stores. In 1907, when the other two principal owners dissolved their partnership, Penney purchased full interest in all three stores. Five years later, in 1912, he was operating 34 stores throughout the Rocky Mountain region. In 1913 he moved the company to Salt Lake City and incorporated it as the J.C. Penny Company. The company continued to be successful and grew to 1400 stores by 1929.

Then the Great Depression hit. The stores faced disastrous declines and James' personal wealth declined greatly. He was able, however, to borrow against his cash value life insurance to keep the company afloat, meet its payroll and cover operating expenses until the economy rebounded. His belief in his company and willingness to risk his personal wealth established J.C. Penney as one of the premier retailers in North America. Today there are 1100 J.C. Penney stores with combined revenues of $18 billion per year.

### The Pampered Chef

Doris Christopher spent most of her time working with homemakers in her suburban Chicago neighborhood during the 1970s. She became convinced that women needed quality, timesaving tools designed to make cooking quicker and easier. To meet her goal, she launched The Pampered  Chef Company by borrowing $3,000 from her life insurance policy to establish her initial inventory. Based on the success of the Tupperware business model, she developed a detailed, multi-level marketing plan and gave birth to her dream.

By 2002, the company had grown into a $700 million operation which caught the attention of Warren Buffett. His company, Berkshire Hathaway, bought The Pampered Chef for $1.5 billion and helped it grow to include 12 million customers today.

 Max and Verda Foster hatched Foster Farms in 1939 by borrowing $1,000 against their life insurance policy. It was enough to invest in an 80-acre farm near Modesto, California. In the beginning, Max worked for the newspaper in Modesto to keep their fledgling business running while Verda focused on raising turkeys. The original hatchery was built right off their bedroom so she could give around-the-clock attention to the eggs and emerging chicks. They eventually expanded to raising both Turkeys and chickens and Max was able to quit his job at the newspaper to focus full-time on the farm. By the 1960s, the company had outgrown the original facility so they moved the corporate headquarters to the small town of Livingston in Central California. Max and Verda's grandson, Ron Foster, continues to run the family business which now boasts more than 10,000 employees and runs operations in California, Oregon, Washington, Colorado and Alabama with products distributed globally.

Any cash value life insurance you hold is a valuable tool with inherent potential. Like the stories you have just read, you may face a situation that needs a little help to keep the dream alive. That help may just be found in the policies in which you have been faithfully investing.

## Section 6

# ANNUITIES

# THE ORIGINS OF ANNUITIES

I trust you are reading this because you are interested in having a plan for your retirement. You can be as creative or conservative as you want with your plan and you have many products from which to choose to implement your strategy. The key to a successful retirement plan is that you believe in it and are comfortable with it. If it helps you reach your goals, makes sense to you and helps raise your confidence in the future, you will be proud of your strategy.

As you evaluate products that will help you prepare for your future, it is likely you will encounter annuities. Many people include annuities in their retirement plan because they offer a distinct advantage over other tools. Annuities allow you to invest large amounts of cash and defer paying on taxes until a later date. It is particularly useful for those close to retirement age who need to catch up because there is no limit to the annual contribution you can make to your annuities. The money you place in an annuity can grow faster because the money you would otherwise pay Uncle Sam remains as part of your balance and continues to earn interest.

### Annuities and the Roman Empire

The idea of an annuity may be new to you but they were being used to do good for people long before you were born. Annuities became a popular option during the Roman Empire. The economy under the Roman emperors flourished which caused many people to prosper. Rather than simply hold onto a lump sum of money, the idea of an "annua" was established. The word "Annua" means "annual payments."[75] Citizens would invest money in this annua in exchange for a promise of lifetime payments which would insure a steady income for the rest of their lives. The transaction was attractive to both buyers and sellers. The buyer gained the security of regular income payments for a known period of time. The seller was able to earn a profit with the built-in potential of paying out less than was accumulated through the length of the contract. This created a classic win/win scenario. Since everybody likes to win, the idea stuck.

As you can imagine, there was an obvious challenge with the plan. No one could predict with certainty exactly how long a client would live. The seller was, therefore, taking a risk that a buyer would live longer than expected. If this happened, more would be paid out over time than the annuity was worth. It is scenarios just like this that led to the innovations that shape our lives. The ambiguity of how long the buyer of an annuity might live gave rise to the first actuarial table in 222 AD. The Roman Scholar Ulpianis created a table displaying the prospective lifespans of all potential annua buyers. For the first time, sellers had a way of determining the terms, interest rate and payouts associated with the contract based on the buyer's expected lifespan. This helped both parties establish a more realistic agreement in which the buyer received long-term income and the seller realized an appropriate profit. The value of the plan was recognized by the Roman government so they established lifetime annuity payments to soldiers as a way of compensating them for their military service.

### Annuities and Europe

During the middle ages, kings, queens and governments could only survive if they found a way to finance an army and amass an arsenal of weapons. The annuity was the financial backbone that enabled England and other European nations to defend their borders and colonize the world. During the 17th century, England and France spent several exhausting and costly years at war with each other. To undergird the government's operation, England created the State Tontine of 1693.[76] The tontine was a special annuity pool that citizens could buy into with an initial lump sum payment. In exchange for their investment, the buyer would receive an annual stipend for the rest of their lives. An attractive innovation was the ability to give their annuities to others (either through a will or a deed) that would last for the lifetime of the nominated survivor as well.

Since the Tontine was a pool, the amount of the annual payout increased each year for the survivor since he or she would receive the funds that would have otherwise gone to the deceased. As each nominee passed, the remaining pool of cash was evenly distributed to a smaller and smaller pool of people. Eventually, the last survivor would receive the entire amount of the remaining principle as a single payout. Since these payouts could grow to be quite large, word spread quickly of the remarkable possibilities of benefiting "lottery style" while enjoying the security aspects of insurance.

Throughout the 16th century, Holland, England as well as other European nations chose to issue annuities rather than government bonds. This decision created large cash reserves that enabled the promised lifetime payments. It also helped fund many government programs and projects. Many of the historic buildings and monuments that still stand today in Europe were made possible with funds from government annuities. Many people have wondered how the lifestyle of England's royal family has been sustained over the centuries. Well, one of the primary reasons is that annuities were established to provide property and income for this highly valued part of English life.

In 1693, the English Parliament created the first charter for the Bank of England which was funded, in part, by the sale of annuities (called shares at the time) that promised a fixed rate of return each year to investors.

Between 1780 and 1880, the British national debt grew consistently as colonies were added and conflicts with other empires continued. The Parliament's need for funds caused the creation, promotions and sale of annuities to expand aggressively. With so many new options hitting the market, people began to be confused about the options and benefits. Something needed to be done to simplify the market. Parliament decided to consolidate its securities into one product called the "Consolidated Annuity." It was nicknamed the "perpetual bond" and became such a popular retirement planning tool that during the late 19th and early 20th century the Consolidated Annuity represented more than half of England's national debt.[77]

## Annuity Timeline

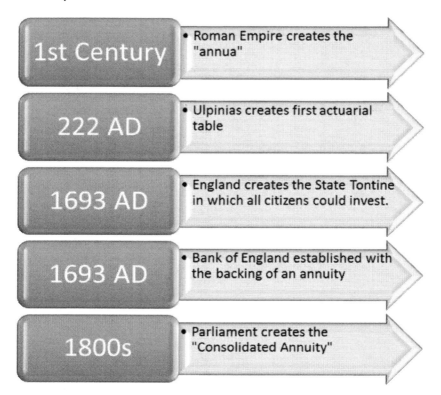

- **1st Century** • Roman Empire creates the "annua"
- **222 AD** • Ulpinias creates first actuarial table
- **1693 AD** • England creates the State Tontine in which all citizens could invest.
- **1693 AD** • Bank of England established with the backing of an annuity
- **1800s** • Parliament creates the "Consolidated Annuity"

# Chapter 18

# ANNUITIES IN AMERICA

D espite the prevalent use of annuities in England, America was relatively slow to incorporate these powerful financial tools. On the eve of the Revolutionary War, the Presbyterian Church began the Corporation for the Relief of Poor and Distressed Presbyterian Ministers and Distressed Widows and Children of Ministers in 1793. I know, it is a very long name but it was a worthy cause. Many of the ministers who were attending to the needs of the colonists served in poor communities with slow economies. They were now approaching retirement age with no means of providing for themselves and their families. Others had died leaving behind widows and children with no way of providing for themselves. Out of a compassionate desire to take care of their own, the church established an annuity to effectively meet the need.

In 1776 the National Pension Program for Soldiers was established. This annuity provided income for soldiers and their families prior to and throughout the Revolutionary War.

**Benjamin Franklin**

Benjamin Franklin may be the brightest example in early American history of the possibilities an annuity can provide. In his will, he assigned a £1,000 annuity to both Boston and Philadelphia. The provisions of the annuity directed the city to lend the money to worthy business apprentices at the going market interest rate for 100 years.[78] Franklin believed that apprentices in the trades would become good citizens. When he outlined the provisions of the annuity, he wrote, "I wish to be useful even after my Death . . . in forming and advancing other young men that may be serviceable to their country."[79] City officials were then to take a portion of the investment to build something of benefit to the city while holding some of the balance for the future. On September 25, 1908, the Franklin Union building was dedicated at the Benjamin Franklin Institute of Technology having been built with funds from the Boston annuity. On May 15, 1916, 900 people took seats in the Franklin Union auditorium to hear guest speaker Alexander Graham Bell on the first ever conference call that linked participants in San Francisco, Chicago, Atlanta, Philadelphia, New York and, of course, Boston. As of 1993, the fund was still worth over $3 million when the city decided to stop taking payments in lieu of a lump sum. The Philadelphia fund did not perform quite as well but still resulted in the development of the Franklin Institute Science Museum and funded loans for tradesmen and vocational training scholarships for two hundred years.

## The War of 1812

In the midst of the War of 1812, a company in Pennsylvania became the first to offer annuities to the general public. Anyone in the country could now take advantage of the benefits of an annuity in their financial planning, even though relatively few pursued the opportunity. The growth of annuities progressed slowly as most Americans throughout the 19th century lived in agrarian communities where extended families managed large family farms or ranches and took care of family members as they aged.

## Civil War

During the Civil War, more of the population began to recognize the value of annuities. The Union Government used annuities to pay soldiers in ongoing payments rather than grant them land. President Abraham Lincoln supported this plan because he saw it as a good way to provide for injured and disabled soldiers as well as their families. The difficult task of adjusting to life with a war induced disability was softened. It should not surprise us because the Civil War in the U.S. gave rise to many of the modern innovations we rely on today:

- Paper money became legal tender for the first time and the federal "greenback" (names for anti-counterfeit green ink used on the back of the notes) replaced paper notes issued by local banks around the country.
- Gail Borden patented condensed milk in 1854 which gave rise to the canned food industry. The war provided a huge market for this type of diet as weary soldiers could enjoy such common favorites as lobster, blueberries, corned beef and ginger cakes.
- Pocket watches became affordable when the Waltham Watch company figured out how to mass produce them with interchangeable parts. The regimented life of the military made these watches popular and made time consciousness a common aspect of western culture.
- Standard shoe sizes. The need to provide gear for a large army made standardizing of shoe sizes and uniforms popular. It was much more efficient than having each solider visit a cobbler or a tailor
- The war made the use of the Telegraph a national phenomenon. The first time in history, "real time" information from generals could get to the President quickly. The communication technology boom that dominates our modern lives was born.
- Farm Machinery became popular. The McCormick Reaper was patented in 1834 and put into production in the 1850s. Adding automation to the farming process enabled "three

farmhands to do the work of 10 or 12. When the war broke out, farm owners in northern wheat-growing states were able to leave their families and go off to war without losing their livelihood," according to Jeremy Atack, professor of history and economics at Vanderbilt University.[80]

## Industrial Revolution

At the end of the 1800s, the industrial revolution drew individuals to the city creating a more mobile society. Family members now lived independently in various parts of the country. As a result, group annuities became popular as a significant part of employers' retirement plans. It enjoyed steady growth until the United States suffered one of the greatest economic disasters in world history – The Great Depression. The trauma of this devastating event created a national desire for security. The motto of the public during the leadership of Franklin D. Roosevelt was "save for a rainy day." As banks began to collapse at an alarming rate, annuities became an attractive means for creating long-term security amidst devastating economic times.

Entrepreneur and educational innovator, Andrew Carnegie developed the Teachers' Pension Fund to support the efforts of American educators. In 1918, the name was changed to the Teachers' Insurance and Annuity Association. We all talk about education being important to our country and to the future of our children. Mr. Carnegie turned his conviction into action by establishing a steady source of income to reward teachers for their investment in the next generation.

## Babe Ruth

A national hero made the use of annuities even more popular. The legendary baseball icon, Babe Ruth, survived the stock market crash of 1929 because he had much of his money in annuities. Sports cartoonist, Christy Walsh, became a friend and business mentor of Ruth and urged him to put his earnings into a lifetime annuity rather than the volatile world of stocks. While many other celebrities were standing in bread lines, the Babe lived well through the Depression. By 1935, he was able to supplement his income with $17,500 per year from his annuities. An adoring public followed suit and annuities became a major force in people's retirement planning. Also in 1935, the largest lifetime income annuity of all time was started, Social Security. Conversations abound of how this fund has been mismanaged or raided for other purposes but the reality is that millions of Americans have enjoyed an improved retirement because of this signature achievement of FDR.

### Modern Developments

In 1952, an educators' retirement fund (TIAA-CREF) became the first organization to offer its members a variable deferred annuity in which they could choose how their funds would be allocated. Investors could now balance the risk they were taking with the potential for higher returns while protecting the balance they had invested.

1986 may be the year that affects you the most when thinking about annuities. The US government passed legislation that gave investors the opportunity to defer their taxes on money they placed in an annuity. This meant they would not have to pay taxes on these funds until they received payments from the annuity. This created an opportunity for greater returns because the money that would have been paid in taxes was now added to the balance. Since the balance was larger, the interest return was also greater. It was obvious the government saw the value of this type of investment because they chose not to limit the amount of money an individual could place in a tax-deferred annuity.

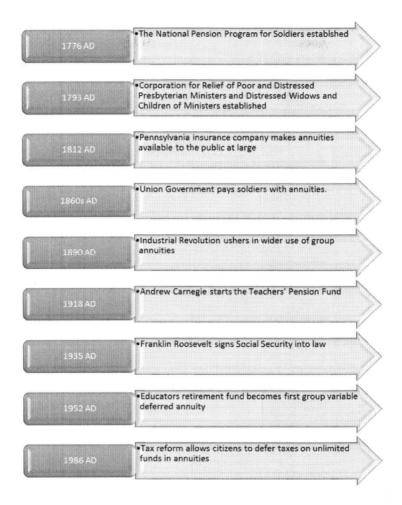

Throughout history, people have used annuities to meet their future financial goals. You are now writing your history. Talk with your financial professional to see if annuities make sense as a part of your plan.

*Chapter 19*

# NEW OPTIONS FOR A CHANGING WORLD

The one thing we all know is everything changes. Every year, new ideas, new research, new phones, new gadgets and new technologies decorate our lives with new possibilities. Charles Purdy, senior editor for Monster.com said, "I don't believe that new needs have been created. We've just created new ways and adopted new technologies to get them done."[81] Consider today's commonplace innovations that were virtually unheard of 20 years ago:

- The IPhone, Android and SmartPhones
- App Developers (More than a million apps have been developed for the interested consumer)
- Google
- Email
- Facebook, Twitter, Blogs and Social Media Managers
- The Cloud (online storage of data)
- GPS
- Wi-Fi and Cell networks

By the time you read this, some of the items on this list may be obsolete and new technologies may have become commonplace that didn't exist when these words were written. That's the nature of the world we live in.

**Indexed Annuities**

We should not be surprised then that newer versions of

annuities have been created. Among the modern innovations in retirement investments is the indexed annuity. It is similar to a fixed annuity because the company guarantees your principal will be protected and sets a fixed term for the contract. It differs in that there is not a fixed rate of return. Instead, your money is linked to one of the major stock market indices, such as the Dow Jones, S&P 500 or the NASDAQ. This type of annuity will allow you to take advantage of the upside potential of the stock market without any of the downside risk. You may be asking yourself, "How would a company do that"? Well the answers are actually very simple. The insurance company will give you certain assurances that make it worth your while to invest. First, the principal of your annuity will never decrease regardless of what happens in the market during the year. Second, if the market increases, your fund will increase also.

At the same time, precautions are built into the annuity that protect everyone involved. The company will "cap" the amount you can earn each year. For example If the index you are linked to grows 11% and you have a "cap" of 6%, the value of your annuity will be increased by 6%. This allows the company to build a reserve to cover the periods of loss in the market thus shielding you and them from the downside risk. Also, the money you deposit with them is never directly invested in the stock market at all. This enables the insurance company to protect your principal so it doesn't decrease during downturns in the market. For instance, if your annuity is linked to the S&P 500 and it tumbles 15% in a terrible year, what do you think will happen to the value of your account? That's right, nothing. In this case zero is your hero! You have given up potentially higher gains in exchange for no losses.

Because the "cap" is generally higher than the guaranteed return of a fixed annuity, an indexed annuity has the potential of yielding a higher return which makes it a great vehicle for accumulating retirement funds. The chart below demonstrates how an indexed annuity with a 6% cap would have performed from 1998 – 2010 compared with the same amount of money invested in a 3% fixed annuity and the S&P 500. As you can see, the indexed annuity during this period would have produced a higher return without experiencing any of the volatility of the market.

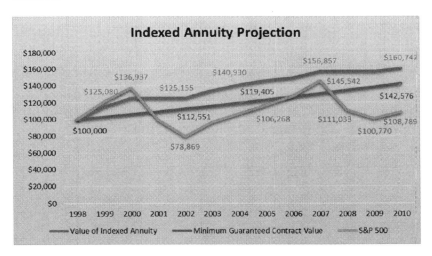

**Indexed Annuity Projection**

## Optional Flexibility

One of the reasons indexed annuities have become popular is their flexibility. They are kind of like an ice cream sundae where you can add the toppings of your choice. Some like to add hot fudge with lots of whipped cream and a cherry. Others like to add fruit toppings and bananas. Still others prefer the simplicity of plain vanilla ice cream. In similar fashion, there are several features that can be added to an indexed annuity.

*Minimum Guarantees.* Indexed annuities can include a minimum guarantee (usually between 1-3% depending on your contract) that comes into play if the index of your investment was flat or declined over the duration of your contract. With this provision, you could be the worst investor in history and your indexed annuity will still earn the guaranteed amount.

*Bonuses.* Many indexed annuities now offer an upfront bonus. These work great if you have had some previous market losses or want to get a jump on your retirement. Bonuses can range from 3% to 10%. That means if you invest $100,000, the insurer will add $3,000 (3%), $5,000 (5%) or $10,000 (10%) to the opening balance. From the beginning, your fund makes more money because the balance is larger. There can be drawbacks, however, because bonuses tend to be offered on longer term contracts. For some of the biggest bonuses you may have to make a commitment of up to 14 years (regulations vary from state to state so check with your advisor). If you are looking for short term returns, the bonus plan will not work well. If, however, you are a long term investor, an indexed annuity with a bonus may be just what you are looking for.

*Penalty Free Withdrawals.* Annuity companies have come to realize what we all know to be true: Life Happens. A popular bumper sticker says, "Life is what happens while we are busy making other plans." For this reason, there are times people need early access to their money.   To facilitate this need, most contracts will allow you to withdraw up to 10% of your account value each year. This won't apply during the first year of your contract because the investment needs time to season but it will be in effect every year after that.

*Income Riders.* One of the most significant innovations in annuities is the introduction of the income rider. The income rider allows you to receive guaranteed income payments for life without giving up control of your money. Prior to income riders, you would simply hand over your money to an insurance company in exchange for a monthly check for the rest of your life. If you managed to live a long time, it was possible you would receive more back from the company than your investment was worth. If, however, you didn't live as long as you anticipated, there could be a sizeable balance which, in some cases, was retained by the insurer. As you can imagine, this left a bad taste in the mouth of many families. Rather than tasting like an ice cream sundae, it was more like sour milk

Insurance companies didn't want customers thinking of them this way so they created Income riders. This innovation was designed to provide peace of mind to individuals who are concerned about outliving their money during retirement, a group that is growing in number every year. According to the Census Bureau, there were 53,364 people over the age of 100 in 2010. That represents more than a 65% increase since 1980. In addition to people living longer, there is a current movement away from traditional pension plans and an uncertain future for Social Security. As a result, more Americans than ever must address the possibility of outliving their retirement nest egg and we are emotional about it. A recent survey conducted by Allianz Life showed that 61% of those surveyed are more concerned about running out of money during retirement then they are of death.[82] So, if you are reasonably confident you will enjoy a lengthy retirement, income riders may be an attractive option for you.

To help you determine if an income rider is wise for you, let's talk a little about how they work. They are similar to a personal pension plan. Like other retirement funds, you deposit a certain amount of money, in this case with an insurance company. They, in turn, will guarantee some level of growth during the life of your annuity. When you plan to retire you will receive a guaranteed lifetime income based on your current age. The payments will continue even after your account value goes to zero. But unlike a pension, income riders allow you to retain complete control over your money. If you decide one day you want to stop the income payments and take the balance as a lump sum, you can do that. And if, God forbid, something were to happen to you, whatever value remains in your fund will be passed to your beneficiaries rather than be retained by the insurer.

Income riders add a level of complexity to your annuity so there are a couple of things you need to consider before concluding this is a good option for you. First, you want be committed to the income payments. Even though there are walkway options, some of the guaranteed growth may be tied to the fact that you will take a lifetime income. Second, the income rider will have fees associated with it, which can be as high as 1%. Just as every topping you put on a sundae costs extra, each provision you add to your annuity will have a fee associated with it. But if outliving your retirement nest egg keeps you up at night, an income rider may be the right solution for you.

### What and When

The two most significant questions you will need to answer in considering an indexed annuity are "What?" and "When?" You have the privilege of choosing "what" index you will link your principal to and "when" the gains will be credited to your account. Because we are talking about money, the company you invest with will provide you options with which they are willing to live. Each insurance company sets up options and limits for how your money responds to the movement in the market and when the interest is actually added to your principal.

For some people, indexed annuities are wise and productive investments. To determine if this is a valuable tool for you, ask lots of questions. Inquire about your choices, the way the company decides what your gains will be, how they add the interest to your account and the limits they will impose. If you don't understand something, ask. If you hear the answer and still don't understand, ask again in a little different way. This is your money and you deserve to know what others are doing with it. It has been estimated that the average person needs to hear something 7 times before it begins to makes sense. It is likely the terms of an indexed annuity are new to you so you will have many more questions than you have answers. Often, the best course of action appears to be a mystery at first but then becomes clear when you understand how things really work.

Consider the college experience of Adam Taggert in a course entitled *Data & Decision-Making*:

**Humans are innately poor at estimating probability** . . . *This was proved to me time and again throughout that course, starting on the very first day. A gifted young professor taught D&D. I was 27 at the time, and he was only a year or two older than me. Given his age, he had a few things to prove to us.*

*As we took our seats for the first time, he asked: "Who wants to bet me $5 that two folks in this room have the same birthday?"*

*We all looked at each other. There were about 65 students, plus the prof. We were all thinking: "365 days in a year. Only 66 people. Those odds don't seem so bad . . ."*

*A hand went up, taking the bet. The prof asked the folks in the back row to start shouting out what their birthday was, one at a time. We got about 6 people in before someone in the middle of the room said, "That's my birthday, too." A $5 bill was passed up to the teacher.*

*"Anyone willing to bet me again?" he asked.*

*Another hand went up, figuring the odds just got much better as the "fluke" overlap had been removed.*

*The exercise repeated. It only took a few more shout outs to hit another shared birthday. Another $5 was handed over.*

*What I later learned was that the professor was making an exceptionally safe bet that only appeared risky because we students were grossly misjudging his probability of being wrong.*

*In fact, as long as there were 57 students left, the*

*prof's* chances of winning the bet were over 99%! *The odds would continue to be overwhelmingly in his favor all the way down to 23 people, at which point they would be 50/50.*[83]

An agent who has your best interest in mind and has studied the field will not mind taking time to answer questions to build your confidence. Be confident enough to keep asking questions until the terms make sense to you.

## Variable Annuities

Some of you reading this are more adventurous than the rest of us. You are riveted to risk, dance with danger and seek out thrills on a regular basis. You are the kind of person who loves stories about places like the "Death Road" outside of La Paz, Bolivia. The road begins at an elevation of 15,400 feet above sea level and is wide enough for about 1 and ½ cars, even though it is described as a two-way road.

From top to bottom is about a 40-mile journey. On one side is a rock face decorated with occasional waterfalls and overhanging trees. On the other side is a sheer drop with few railings and no fences. Needless to say, if you fall off, it is highly unlikely you will experience any other adventures! In 1994, the Inter-American Development Bank conducted a study revealing that 200-300 people die on this road annually and proclaimed it was the World's Most Dangerous Road.

Despite the dangers, more than 25,000 mountain bike riders are drawn to the challenge each year. The first 12 ½ miles of the ride is tarmac which gives the cyclists a great opportunity to take in the majestic Amazon landscape. The rest is a four hour trek on gravel and dirt which jars every part of your body and makes your hands numb. All the while, you have to maintain intense focus so you don't end up as a death road statistic.

Adam, an avid traveler with a relentless drive for adventure, described his ride as, "Quite literally the most fun I've ever had doing anything." Andrew, who describes himself as a Teacher on Two Wheels, recounts his experience, "riding a full suspension mountain bike for hours down The Death Road is an awesome thing to do. Finishing the ride with your life intact is like doing that Keanu Reeves Haha-you-can't-kill-me dance in the Matrix where he misses all the bullets flying by in slo-mo . . ." He even lists reasons why he believes this is a good idea:

1. The scenery is spectacular.
2. At times, the adrenaline is so potent and intoxicating you're left wondering how it is that governments haven't yet outlawed the stuff.
3. You use someone else's expensive bike!
4. Assuming you survive, you're left with that immortal wizard feeling at the end–a feeling hard to come by in 'normal' daily life . . . unless, of course, you do things in your normal daily life that allow you to shake hands with Death

and then slap him firmly in the face.[84]

If you are one of those thrill seekers who loves opportunities like this, you will likely be drawn to variable annuities. They possess great potential, carry significant risk and are, by their nature, complex. Mark Cussen, CFP, CMFC, AFC and contributor to Investopedia states, "They [variable annuities] are one of the most complex investments in existence, probably second only to the variable universal life insurance." The nature of variable annuities mean they are subject to regulation by the Securities and Exchange Commission (SEC). An agent who offers you a variable annuity must be licensed to sell life insurance in your state and must be registered with the National Association of Securities Dealers (NASD). This is required because the risk is high with the corresponding possibility of higher returns.

Most people shy away from these types of options because they prefer a more cautious approach and lean toward indexed annuities. Some people, however, like the freedom to make choices and the adventure of seeking greater returns. In a variable annuity, you will be offered a number of options for investing your principal. Each of these options (called subaccounts) have varying levels of risk and earning potential. You decide how much of your balance is placed in each of these subaccounts. As your circumstances or investment goals change, you can adjust how your funds are allocated. Along with this increased flexibility, you will take on the market risks of the stock and bond funds tied to your annuity. Your account will be very similar to a mutual fund and will either grow or shrink with the market. You may succeed greatly with this type of annuity because the stock and bond markets have seasons of positive growth. You may also suffer "accidents" when the market goes through a season of deep losses. In a variable annuity, the value of your investment will follow the market for good and bad.

In addition to the market risks associated with variable annuities there can be substantial fees involved. Each subaccount will have a fee on top of a charge known as an M&E fee or Mortality and Expense fee which is used to cover death benefits and administrative expenses. Many of these contracts also offer additional riders that, you guessed it, comes with another fee. When you add all of the fees together they can total up to more than 3% annually.   Keep in mind these fees will be charged whether your account is up or down for the year and can have a huge impact to the growth of your annuity.

If you choose to take this journey, you are going to want a guide. In Bolivia, you are not allowed on the Death Road without a guide who is familiar with the journey. There are too many hazards and too many surprises to allow inexperienced riders to go it alone.

Variable annuities are the same way. There are too many options and too much complexity for an individual investor to keep track of the nuances. Look for an agent who is willing to partner with you, strategize with you and help you grasp the implications of your choices. This type of adviser will approach you as an intelligent, courageous competitor in the financial arena and will help you discern if the options you are considering are recklessly ridiculous or brilliantly in your favor.

**Section 7**

---

# LONG TERM CARE

*Chapter 20*

# IT'S PERSONAL

E d was excited to be surrounded by his kids and grandkids on his 85th birthday. Despite the effects of the stroke he suffered in his late forties, he has managed to remain independent and live at home. He was told by his doctor at the beginning of the year that he had to stop taking medication for osteoporosis because of potential side effects. Ed took it as good news since his bone density test showed improvements over the past two years.

A few months after the family celebration, Ed hurt his back. It was just a simple movement in his bedroom but the pain became so great he had to call 911. After two visits to the emergency room and a consultation with his doctor, he was diagnosed with a fractured vertebra. The pain and subsequent decrease in regular daily movement further hindered his abilities. He was no longer able to get out of bed on his own, shower himself or get himself dressed.

He wasn't admitted to the hospital by his doctor so his Medicare benefits would not cover a rehabilitation facility. Medicare requires a three day hospital stay before those benefits are available so Ed had to put together his own plan. The family arranged for home health care each morning to assist him with getting dressed but it became quickly evident that he needed more help.

One of Ed's grandsons volunteered to stay with him for two weeks during a break in his school schedule. It turned out to be a good thing because he required daily assistance with showering and dressing. He also needed "coaching" to keep him on schedule with a new exercise routine set up by his physical therapist. Every four hours around the clock, they did exercises from his chair. Twice a day, they walked 50 – 100 feet which was a slow process involving a walker, a ramp and a healthy dose of patience.

Ed is fortunate because his mind is still sharp and, being a retired engineer, he did the math on what it would have cost him to bring in home health care to do what his grandson had done. Being a resident of Southern California, he figured out it would cost him about $3500 per month.

Years ago he invested in a life insurance policy that includes a long term care provision. He knew the provisions would not become available until he was "qualified" for 90 days but the fracture in his back was a good reminder of why he acquired this coverage in the first place. He is still hoping to never need the coverage but he is glad it is in his portfolio. He feels good that his policy will provide money for his loved ones when his life is over. And, he has a renewed sense of relief that this policy is in place should circumstances present the need for greater care.

### What does it take to be "Qualified?"

Can I state the obvious? We are all emotional about needing help. We have built our careers and created a satisfying life through hard work and independence. We are used to taking care of ourselves and making ourselves available to help others. None of us have the goal of needing significant assistance.

If your parents are getting older, this is especially difficult to accept. We have all grown used to relying on our parents. They have been strong for most of our lives. They provided for us when we were children. They advised us when we were young adults. They taught us, warned us, encouraged us and held us up. It is hard to picture that these rocks of stability could ever need help with basic activities of life.

As a result, we approach the need for end of life

care from a very personal perspective. We deny the need for it at first and then demand the need gets covered quickly and abundantly. Those who provide coverage can't be quite this subjective so there is a standard that determines when someone is qualified to receive the benefits contained in Medicaid or a private policy.

In simple form, a person is considered eligible for long term care when he or she needs assistance with at least two "activities of daily living." These activities include:

*Bathing*: Involves grooming activities such as shaving, brushing your teeth and arranging your hair.

*Dressing*: Involves choosing appropriate garments to wear, dressing and undressing, having no trouble with buttons, zippers or other fasteners.

*Eating*: Involves the ability to feed yourself.

*Transferring*: Includes the ability to walk, or, if not ambulatory, being able to transfer yourself from your bed or chair to a wheelchair and back.

*Continence*: Involves being able to control your bowels and bladder, or manage alternative methods of incontinence independently.

*Toileting*: Involves being able to use the toilet and practice healthy hygiene.

It is awkward and embarrassing to diagnose whether you are qualified for long term care. It will become an issue for almost all of us so it is wise to become more comfortable with the topic now. As you consider your own need to be prepared for issues of aging, consider the following facts:

- The average American expects to live until age 79 or beyond.[85] To put this in perspective, the average male expected to live about 48 years in 1900 and about 67 years in 1960.[86] Today, we are the peak of our lives when people in the past were winding down.
- In 2005 there were 37 million Americans who were age 65 or older.
- By 2050, it is expected that there will be 81 million Americans in that same age category.
- In 2012, 9 million Americans needed long-term care.
- By 2020, that number is expected to rise to 12 million.
- 78% of elderly Americans who need long-term care receive it from family members or close friends. As a result, approximately 34 million Americans are caregivers to someone age 50 or older. This is about the same number of people who live in the entire state of California (38 million), the most populous state in the U.S. It is also equivalent to the population of the entire country of Canada. (35 million). In other words, it is a lot of people.
- In order to be eligible for long-term benefits

provided by Medicaid, a healthy spouse can have no more than $113,640 worth of assets.

- 79 is the average age at which an elderly person is admitted to a nursing home.
- 40% of Americans who reach age 65 will be admitted to a nursing home at some time in their life and will stay for an average of 892 days (2.44 years).
- The average age of an individual who purchased long-term care insurance in 2010 was 59.[87]

All of us are going to be affected in some way by the aging process. We can't stop it and we can't choose when it will move from being a hassle to being a life changing hindrance. Still, most people try to ignore the inevitable. "67% of people who are planning to have someone help with care have not asked them and one in five caregivers said they are 'not at all prepared.'"[88] Add to this that the National Alliance for Caregiving reports one in five caregivers provide more than 40 hours per week of care.[89] That is a lot of time for someone who is not prepared!

### The New Boom of the Baby Boom

The baby boom represents the 76.4 million people born between 1946 and 1964. Apparently everyone was excited to build their families after World War II because in 1946 3.4 million babies were born—the biggest one year addition to the population in history. That was followed by 3.8 million in 1947, 3.9 in 1952 and more than 4 million per year from 1954 to 1964. By their sheer size, the baby boom has impacted life through every stage of their growth. They are responsible for the growth of suburbs, the rise of opportunities for women and minorities, the credit explosion, the rise of the media and the dominance of technology. Baby boomers have always been a confident group who have integrated new innovations throughout their lives. As a result, they live longer and have higher expectations than previous generations.

Now they are getting older and they are going to need care. "By 2020, due to the rapid retirement of baby-boomers, approximately one in three workers will be faced with providing some form of Long Term Care for their boomer parents."[90] And by 2030, about one in five Americans will be older than 65.[91] Many of them will experience remarkably good health while others will face debilitating diseases or life altering characteristics of aging.

Baby Boomers are an educated lot so many of them have been researching solutions to end of life care and investing in products to help them with the transition. It is still the case, however, that most people rely on family for the assistance they need. "For every one person receiving long term care in a nursing home, there are four people receiving home health care."[92] As families become increasingly fractured and spread out around the country, policies that help cover costs have been trending up. Genworth, the largest long term care insurance company in America, reports the following behaviors by those with long term care coverage:

- 43% of claims lasted less than 1 year.
- The average length of a claim that lasted more than a year was 3.9 years.
- 15% of their claims have lasted longer than 5 years.
- Their longest claim lasted 18.7 years
- The youngest person they made payments to was 27 years old.
- The oldest person they made payments to was 103.[93]

## Making Preparations

One thoughtful woman on the Suddenly Senior website reminds us all of the value of being prepared. She notes that many baby boomers have chosen to settle in Florida for their retirement years. In the same way that aging is inevitable, hurricanes are inevitable in this great southern state so she recommends the following precautions:

*Evacuation Route:* If you live in a low-lying area, you should have an evacuation route planned out. (To determine whether you live in a low-lying area, look at your driver's license; if it says "Florida," you live in a low-lying area.) The purpose of having an evacuation route is to avoid being trapped in your home when a major storm hits. Instead, you will be trapped in a gigantic traffic jam several miles from your home, along with two hundred thousand other evacuees. So, as a bonus, you will not be lonely.

*Hurricane Supplies:* If you don't evacuate, you will need a mess of supplies. Do not buy them now! Florida tradition requires that you wait until the last possible minute, then go to the supermarket and get into vicious fights with strangers over who gets the last can of cat food. In addition to food and water, you will need the following supplies:

- 23 flashlights. At least $167 worth of batteries that turn out, when the power goes off, to be the wrong size for the flashlights.
- Bleach. (No, I don't know what the bleach is for. NOBODY knows what the bleach is for, but it's traditional, so GET some!)
- A big knife that you can strap to your leg. (This will be useless in a hurricane, but it looks cool.)
- A large quantity of raw chicken, to placate the alligators. (Ask anybody who went through Andrew; after the hurricane, there WILL be irate alligators.)
- $35,000 in cash or diamonds so that, after the hurricane passes, you can buy a generator from a man with no discernible teeth.

Of course these are just basic precautions. As the hurricane draws near, it is vitally important that you keep abreast of the situation by turning on your television if you have a generator that's working to keep the TV going and watching TV reporters in rain slickers stand right next to the ocean and tell you over and over how vitally important it is for everybody to stay away from the ocean. Good luck and remember: It is great living in Paradise.[94]

The way you prepare is up to you but it is in your best interest to be prepared!

*Chapter 21*

# WHAT IS IT?

L ong term care is a progressive term. What I mean is that it can move from simple and casual to complex and intense. Most people need progressively more help as they age so we can't talk about long term care as just one thing. Although taking care of an aging loved one is as unique to each family as the family itself, the type of assistance we will need falls into a number of different categories:

*Personal Caretakers*: In many cases, there is a compassionate family member who has the willingness and time to provide personal assistance. This is, of course, cheaper than paying someone to provide the same help. It is, however, a significant commitment on the part of the caregiver so the intangible costs of stress, loss of time and personal sacrifice of other goals must be considered.

*Homemaker Services*: Most people want to live in their own homes as long as possible. At some age, however, the daily needs of living on your own can become a burden that goes beyond your strength or ability. Homemaker services offer in-home help to complete "hands-off" care such as cooking, house cleaning, social companionship or running errands. This service does not include helping with hygiene needs or any medical services.

*Home Health Aide Services*: This is "hands-on" assistance that includes personal care such as bathing, dressing, personal grooming, monitoring prescription schedules and helping with routines assigned by physical or occupational therapists. This is the in-home alternative to a residential care facility or nursing home.

*Adult Day Health Care*: People of all ages long to be connected with others. Through work, clubs, religious organizations and hobbies, people interact with others who are like-minded and share common interests. Part of the aging process includes a greater challenge to stay connected. Loss of mobility, restrictions to driving and limited capabilities make it impossible to keep the same schedule as before. One solution is involvement in adult day care activities. Most communities include supervised facilities that provide daily activities and social interaction to senior adults which can provide a much needed break for caregivers. Some facilities will even provide personal care services, transportation, medication management, guidance for social services and therapeutic activities to help adults maintain physical conditioning and confidence.

*Assisted Living Facility*: This is an intermediate care complex for those who need assistance with daily living activities, such as cooking or cleaning, and have decided it is better to live in a facility than try to work it out at home. Residents at an assisted living facility maintain a high level of independence and live active lifestyles in community with others. This is made possible by the minimal assistance they receive with everyday tasks.

*Nursing Home Care*: Eventually we all get to the point where we cannot take care of ourselves. It can range from assistance with everything to needing help in specific vital areas. An option that works for many senior adults is a nursing home. These residences offer personal care assistance, room and board, and consistent supervision. They also administer medication, therapies and rehabilitation regiments along with skilled nursing care 24 hours per day.

## What Do These Options Cost?

The question we all want answered is impossible to put in simple terms that apply to everyone. The price depends on where you live and how much help you need. For planning purposes, however, we can discuss the range of costs across the country. The numbers listed below are based upon Genworth's 2014 Cost of Care Survey which includes information from all 50 states.[95] The yearly figures assume full-time care even though I understand sometimes only part-time care is necessary. As you anticipate the type of care for which you might need to take advantage, these figures can provide a place to start.

Homemaker Services — Highest State Cost = $39 per hour; $89,232 per year — Lowest State Cost = $8 per hour; $18,304 per year — National Median = $19 per hour; $43,472 per year

Home Health Aide — Highest State Cost = $39 per hour; $89,232 per year — Lowest State Cost = $9 per hour; $20,592 per year — National Median = $20 per hour; $45,188 per year

Adult Day Care — Highest State Cost = $215 per day; $55,900 per year — Lowest State Cost = $12 per day; $3,120 per year — National Median = $65 per day; $16,900 per year

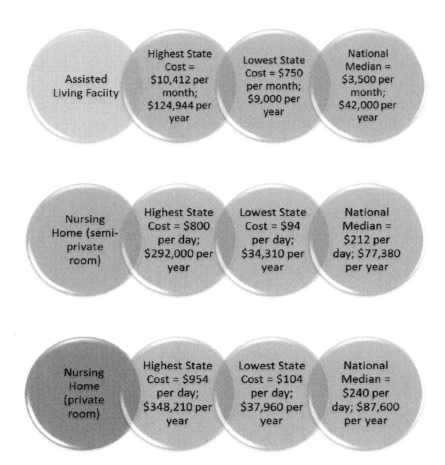

## Strategic Questions

Long term care insurance is a different breed from life insurance, health insurance or auto insurance. Most people would agree that everyone needs these forms of coverage and in some cases it is even mandated by law. Long term care coverage is a personal decision that is extremely good for some and unnecessary for others. As you consider whether this is a good option for you, you will want to ask yourself (and others you trust) the following questions:

- *What is my tolerance for risk?* If you obtain insurance, you will gain a sense of security when it comes to debilitating health issues. You will also take the risk that you may never need to use it. If you choose not to obtain a policy, whatever care you end up needing will come out of your pocket. Which risk sounds more attractive to you?
- *Does the insurance you are considering makes sense?*
  - Is the benefit amount per day compatible with costs in your area? (Standard options range from $100 to $400 per day. You can research costs in your state at genworth.com/costofcare).
  - *Will this policy provide benefits for the length of time that makes sense to you?* Standard options include 24, 36, 48, 60 or 72 months. The national average for how long people need long term care is just under 2 ½ years. This, however, is simply the average. You may need help for a longer or shorter time. To make an intelligent decision, you will need information from your family background, your own health history, your personal level of determination to live independently and the support you can realistically anticipate from your family or close friends.
  - *How long will you have to cover your own expenses before insurance begins to pay out?* This is what insurance companies refer to as the elimination period. Standard options include 30, 90, 180 or 360 days.
  - *Are you interested in inflation protection?* One thing we can all be sure of is that care will cost more 10 years from now than it does today. Therefore, the coverage you will need in the future is different than what you would need today. Do you want to cover the inflationary cost by putting money away or do you want to include this in your policy?

- *What is your most important reason for considering long term care insurance?*
  - Are you seeking the security of knowing you have coverage?
  - Are you trying to protect your assets for your heirs?
  - Are you wanting to avoid being a burden on your kids?

**What is Your Plan?**

The need for long term care is inescapable because we are all aging. We would all like to feel young forever and experience great health until we are 100 years old. The reality is most of us will face a season of life where we need significant assistance. And, this help is inconvenient, awkward and embarrassing. No one wants to admit they need help bathing, using the toilet, dressing or eating. It is also in nobody's plans to face Alzheimer's, Dementia or some other life altering illness. We do not, however, have the luxury of putting our heads in the sand and ignoring the possibility.

Like other critical areas of life, each of us needs a plan for addressing the long term care needs we are likely to be confronted with. So, what is your plan? The most common plan I hear is wishful thinking.

*I exercise regularly so I am just going to keep running until the end and leave the nursing home to others.*

*Everyone in my family lives long without serious troubles.*

*My kids loves me. They will take care of me.*

*I am going to go out with a bang. No long term agony for me. I will just have a heart attack or a car accident and be done.*

*The government will take care of me if I run out of money.*

*My spouse would never allow me to be neglected.*

These statements are, of course, true for some people. But, there is no way to predict if they will be true for us so each of us needs to develop a plan.

# Chapter 22

# CLIMB THE HILL TOGETHER

The most satisfying option for long term care, if everyone is agreeable to it, is for family members to take care of each other. We would all prefer to live at home surrounded by people who love us and are willing to offer compassionate assistance. Most families, however, have never had this conversation. We are either afraid of the discussion, living in denial or believe that everyone else wants to ignore the issue. Forming a plan that makes sense begins with scheduling a time to talk with your family.

**Let's Talk!**

Talking about long term care and end of life issues is stressful for everyone so it is wise to be flexible and determined. Be flexible enough to allow everyone involved to have different reactions and be determined enough to keep approaching the discussion until real decisions have been reached.

Irene's daughter and son-in-law were loyal during her journey with a terminal illness. They moved in with her, transported her to various doctor appointments and helped manage her hospice care. I was impressed with their level of care and compassion.

I was equally surprised one day while we were meeting to discuss her affairs. He abruptly stood up and threw his chair at a window. We all bolted upright in our chairs as our heads snapped to attention.

He then pointed at this mother-in-law and blurted out, "It should have been you!"

"What are you talking about?" I shot back at him.

"I just found out I have a terminal disease. I chose not to move out West because we needed to take care of her," pointing again at his mother-in-law.

"It was supposed to be you, not me!"

Things can get pretty intense when end of life issues are at hand, so be prepared. As you talk with family you may get any or all of the following responses:[96]

*An open willingness to talk about the issues.* Some members of your family have been wanting to have this conversation because they like a direct, "face up" approach to life's issues. These members of your inner circle will participate enthusiastically, ask clarifying questions and offer potential solutions.

*Denial.* Some members of your family simply do not want to talk about the possibility that you may die or have significant medical challenges. They see you as strong, capable and trustworthy. They depend upon you and want to believe you will be strong for them for the rest of their lives. Deep down they know this is not true but they want to believe it anyway.

*Glazed over eyes.* These are members of your family who appear to be listening with interest but in reality are ignoring the reality of the discussion and will probably forget most of what is talked about.

*Conveniently distracted.* Other members of your family will suddenly find other "important" things that need to be done at the same time as your scheduled conversation. The grass needs to be mowed, errands need to be run, friends need to be met or neglected home chores need to be done now. For this reason, it may take more than one meeting to work through the plan.

*Nervous laughter.* Some of the people you love relieve stress by laughing or making light of serious situations. It is really not a problem as long as progress is being made in the conversation.

### Climb the H.I.L.L. Together

**H**it the target. Talking about aging, dying, chronic medical issues and loss of freedom is not pleasant for anyone. As a result, people are nervous and hesitant. You can make it easier on everyone by having a positive attitude, sharing your dreams for the future and clearly laying out your objectives in planning for your future. This sets a positive tone for the whole process and gives everyone a worthwhile goal to focus on.

**I**nvestigate options. There is no one "right" way to address the need for long term care or the tools you will employ to meet the needs. It is, therefore, wise to identify as many options as you can. This also provides the more hesitant people in your circle time to adjust. The more options you are willing to consider, the more confidence you will have in the choices you make.

**L**isten to everyone. The people you have invited to this meeting are important to you and care about you. They all have opinions, concerns and insights to share. They all need to feel important in the process and you never know when the best course of action will come from an unexpected source.

**L**et it linger. These are important, far-reaching decisions so you don't have to decide everything at one meeting. Some of your loved ones may need time to digest the implications and options. Developing an effective plan that everyone understands and buys into is more important than being efficient with your planning process.

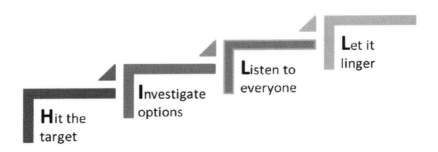

## Why people don't buy LTC

Despite the fact that everyone will be faced with elderly challenges, many people refuse to think about or to invest in any solutions that will provide for the needs they know are coming. The obvious question is, "Why?" Why would intelligent, hard-working people choose to ignore a need they know is inevitable?

I am not asking this question to criticize anyone because the issues we are talking about are emotional, personal and challenging to an already overstretched budget. So, let's explore together some of the well-meaning reasons people choose not to pursue coverage.

*It seems too expensive.* Investing in a long term care policy is an additional cost to whatever else you are doing to save for retirement. When you consider the amount of money you are already putting in savings, adding to your 401(k), depositing in an IRA, it is easy to conclude that the funds you have available for your future are already fully committed. The thought of taking more from your current budget for the possibility that you may have trouble in the future can be hard to envision.

*It doesn't seem necessary.* If you have a history of good health in your family and are in good shape, it is easy to conclude you are going to experience good health for a long, long time. We all tend to be confident about our abilities and opportunities and we need to be. In order to be successful in our careers and families we need to believe in ourselves and the skills we have developed. If we don't believe that self-discipline, hard work and healthy decisions will work for us, we will lose momentum and fail in our goals. The very confidence that enables us to succeed can keep us from believing we need to be concerned about long term care.

*It may not seem like a good investment.* Since long term care insurance is insurance, there is no guarantee we will get our investment back. It is possible that you will buy coverage but never end up using it. On the one hand, this would be a good thing because it means you have maintained good health throughout your life. You have had the physical strength to enjoy your elderly years the way you wanted. On the other hand, this means the money you put into coverage will never be used and there are no refunds on policies such as this.

*I am not sure I can trust those who provide long term care insurance.* Although this type of coverage has its roots in compassion for critical needs of elderly Americans, many people are suspicious of the motives in the industry. It is easy to conclude that insurance companies are trying to take advantage of a highly emotional need in the lives of families. The benefit is only tangible if you or a loved one cannot fully take care of yourself at some potential time in the future. And, I do want to admit that policies in the past have had their problems. Many of them did not have provisions for inflation built in and were structured to have premiums rise as costs rise. As a result, the policy cost more and more the longer you held the policy. If it turned out that you did not need the benefits, it left a bad taste in people's mouths after having invested greater amounts of money. Newer products have safeguards against this kind of outcome so that you gain some investment value from the policy.

*I would do better self-insuring.* If you have done well in your life, it may seem like a better idea to provide for your own care rather than rely on an insurance company to control the money for your long term care. If you are disciplined and careful to safeguard the money you have set aside for long term care, this may be an option for you. It is harder, however, when you actually start writing checks for sizeable amounts of money. It can get very emotional for family members to see that much money going out of the bank each and every month. Most families are not really prepared for this type of experience so long term care coverage relieves the emotional stress. Since newer products help safeguard the investment you are making, it makes more sense than ever to consider having insurance for your long term care needs.

*I don't understand the industry.* You are busy with your career and family and don't spend time studying insurance products. Even though products are being updated every year and new alternatives are being added, it is unlikely you are aware of the range of solutions available to you. If all you think of when you consider long term care is the basic type of policy where you pay a premium for benefits you may or may not ever use, you may dismiss the discussion before it ever really begins.

## Welcome the Surprises

When you take time to discuss these issues with the people you love, you may encounter some surprising responses, like the woman who wanted to teach her child to be compassionate toward the aging.

> *While working for an organization that delivers lunches to elderly shut-ins, I used to take my four-year-old daughter on my afternoon rounds. She was unfailingly intrigued by the various appliances of old age, particularly the canes, walkers and wheelchairs.*

> *One day I found her staring at a pair of false teeth soaking in a glass. As I braced myself for the inevitable barrage of questions, she merely turned and whispered, "The tooth fairy will never believe this!"*[97]

Some of the responses you encounter will be difficult and some will be humorous. Either way, it is good to have the people we love in the discussion.

# Chapter 23

# HYBRIDS CAN HELP

Newer products have come into play over the past few years to address the changing landscape of long term care. These new tools have appropriately been called hybrid policies. I find this fascinating because many other areas of our lives are enhanced by hybrids. The most common hybrids most of us incorporate into our lives come from the kitchen.

Take bananas, for instance. Natural bananas tend to vary in size which make them hard to process and package. They are also prone to diseases that can threaten the entire worldwide crop. Hybrids have turned this popular yellow fruit into a global favorite. Some of the more interesting facts about bananas include:

- Bananas are one of the healthier natural food sources in the world, ounce for ounce. They contain almost no fat; are very low in calories; and are high in vitamin B6, fiber, and potassium. They also contain decent amounts of phosphorus, magnesium, calcium, iron, selenium, manganese, copper, zinc, Vitamin A, Vitamin B1, Vitamin B2, Niacin, Folate, Vitamin C, Vitamin E, Vitamin K, and Pantothenic Acid. Bananas are also known to lower the risk of heart attacks and strokes, as well as decrease your risk of getting cancer, according to the FDA.

- Americans eat more bananas than any other fruit, with an average consumption of 26.2 pounds of bananas per

American per year. In fact, Americans eat more bananas than apples and oranges combined.

- Banana leaves are waterproof and generally very large. As such, in certain parts of the world, they are used as disposable plates and food containers. They also are often steamed with other foods; the juices from the leaves protect the food from burning and give the food a sweet flavor. These leaves also make great umbrellas.
- Today there are about 70 million people in the world who depend on the banana as one of their primary food sources, as well as the plant's uses in making clothing, paper, and other common household products.[98]

Almonds are another pervasive hybrid. They are rich in magnesium, monounsaturated fat, full-spectrum vitamin E and are abundant. Although California is the only place in North America where almonds are grown commercially, they rank as the seventh largest U.S. food export. More than 450,000 acres in the lush San Joaquin and Sacramento valleys are under almond cultivation, stretching 400 miles between Bakersfield and Red Bluff, California. Almonds are California's largest tree nut crop in total dollar value and acreage. Approximately 6,000 almond growers produce 100 percent of the commercial domestic supply and more than 70 percent of worldwide production. Over 90 nations import California almonds.[99]

The popularity of almonds, however, is only possible because of the hybrid process. Wild almonds (referred to as bitter almonds) contain high levels of amygdalin, a potent glycoside that the body metabolizes into hydrogen cyanide. An alternative cancer treatment called laetrile, or "vitamin B17," uses amygdalin as the active ingredient, and patients who've taken it often suffer cyanide poisoning. Early farmers discovered a common genetic mutation that prevented wild almonds from producing amygdalin which gave rise to "sweet" almonds which are the non-toxic, delicious nuts we all enjoy.

In addition to bananas and almonds, other popular hybrid foods include boysenberries (a hybrid of the raspberry, loganberry and blackberry), loganberry (blackberry and European red raspberry), marionberry (cross between the Chehalem and Olallieberry), grapefruit (pummelo and sweet orange), broccollini (a cross between broccoli and Chinese kale), and most apples (Braeburn, Macintosh, Red Delicious, Gala, Fuji, Pink Lady, Golden Delicious).

## Hybrids on the Road

Hybrids have also become common place on American highways. Not everybody is a fan of hybrids but they are here to stay because many drivers like the combination of benefits that result when you put a gasoline engine and an electric motor into one vehicle. Some of the uses of hybrid technology include:

*Regenerative Braking.* The electric motor applies resistance to the drivetrain causing the wheels to slow down. In return, the energy from the wheels turns the motor, which functions as a generator, converting energy normally wasted during coasting and braking into electricity, which is stored in a battery until needed by the electric motor.

*Electric Motor Drive/Assist.* The electric motor provides additional power to assist the engine in accelerating, passing, or hill climbing. This allows a smaller, more efficient engine to be used. In some vehicles, the motor alone provides power for low-speed driving conditions where internal combustion engines are least efficient.

*Automatic Start/Shutoff.* Automatically shuts off the engine when the vehicle comes to a stop and restarts it when the accelerator is pressed. This prevents wasted energy from idling.[100]

Hybrid vehicles are not really new as they have been around for a while in other applications. Most of the locomotives we see pulling trains are diesel-electric hybrids. Submarines are also hybrid vehicles -- some are nuclear-electric and some are diesel-electric.[101] Toyota (with the Prius) and Honda (with the insight) introduced hybrids as viable options for American drivers. Since then almost every auto manufacturer has added a hybrid option to its lineup.

Hybrid vehicles are certainly more complicated than traditional gas powered vehicles. The question naturally arises then, "Why would people want to drive a hybrid?" The answer is, they reduce tailpipe emissions and get better gas mileage. The owner of a hybrid car will spend less money on gasoline at the pump and will live with the satisfying feeling that they are helping to make the planet a better and safer place.

## Hybrid LTC Policies

Just as there are hybrid fruits and vegetables that enhance our lives and hybrid cars that are changing the way we think about transportation, there are hybrid policies that can help in your planning for long term care. Hybrid foods and cars were created to address obvious problems. In the same way, innovative people saw the need for better coverage for long term care. Companies now combine the best of life insurance with the best of long term care coverage or they combine the benefits of an annuity with the assurance of long term care coverage. Although thousands of people had already purchased long term care policies, industry professionals realized we could do better. Individuals were not just concerned about their need for care as they grew older. They were equally concerned about the impact of inflation and taxes on their income. In addition, they often think about the legacy they are going to leave their family. The belief that these concerns could be addressed at the same time gave rise to the hybrid.

In this day and age of constant information and technological independence, the average citizen is looking for a comprehensive plan with simple solutions that are flexible enough to cover a range of possible outcomes in their lives. In other words, most people aren't looking for a long term care policy that only provides long term care. They want a policy that can address long term medical issues if necessary but they also want it to provide investment value for themselves or their families, and they want it to return money to the family if they are fortunate enough to maintain good health.

The first popular type of hybrid is a life insurance policy with a long term care rider or a chronic illness rider. The life insurance you hold has a defined death benefit. The rider allows you to access the benefit as an advance if you face the need for intense care. After making "withdrawals" to cover costs of care, the remaining amount will be available to your heirs.

Let's say you decide on a life insurance policy with a death benefit of $500,000. You make provisions when you buy the policy to make $300,000 available for long term care. Most policies require you to decide when you buy how much will be allocated and how much per month you can withdraw if the need arises. You estimate that covering three years of long term care at $100,000 per year would be sufficient. Let's then say you actually need to use the provision for one year. That would mean you advanced $100,000 to address your living needs leaving $400,000 to your heirs. The same policy has addressed two different needs.

The other popular type of hybrid is an annuity with a long term care rider. An annuity is a financial tool set up to make regular payments to you beginning at a certain age and continuing for the rest of your life. If you add long term care coverage to the annuity, it gives you flexibility of accessing the money sooner than you normally would if you need acute assistance with daily activities. If you have a standalone annuity, you could make accelerated withdrawals from the policy but the funds would be taxable. If you divert these funds to long term care, the funds will fall under the provisions of the 2010 Pension Protection Act and will be available without tax consequence. Whether you use the annuity funds for normal daily living or you access them for long term care, whatever cash value is left in the policy at the end of your life will go to whoever you have assigned as the beneficiary.

Let's say you own an annuity that is worth $500,000 which is set up to pay $3000 per month beginning at age 70 and you are privileged to live until 86 years old. If you remain healthy, you will receive the $3000 each and every month and will likely still have approximately $500,000 in cash value that will be passed on to your loved ones. Let's assume for the moment you experience physical setbacks and end up needing long term care for two years. Let's also assume that care costs you $65,000 per year. If you have a long term care rider on your annuity, you can step up your payments to cover this cost without experiencing any penalties. The cash value of your annuity will be worth less at the end of your life but you will still leave approximately 350,000 to the people you care about. The hybrid nature of this type of coverage allows you to meet both goals with a high level of flexibility.

## As Versatile as an Apron

A good long term policy is a lot like a grandma's apron. The Suddenly Senior website reminds all of us that grandma's apron was one of the most versatile tools ever devised. The principle use of Grandma's apron was to protect the dress underneath, but along with that, it served a number of different purposes:

- It was a holder for removing hot pans from the oven.
- It was wonderful for drying children's tears, and on occasion was even used for cleaning out dirty ears.
- From the chicken-coop, the apron was used for carrying eggs, fussy chicks, and sometimes half-hatched eggs to be finished in the warming oven.
- When company came, those aprons were ideal hiding places for shy kids.
- When the weather was cold, grandma wrapped it around her arms.
- Those big old aprons wiped many a perspiring brow, bent over the hot wood stove.
- Chips and kindling wood were brought into the kitchen in that apron.
- From the garden, it carried all sorts of vegetables. After the peas had been shelled, it carried out the hulls.
- In the fall, the apron was used to bring in apples that had fallen from the trees.
- When unexpected company drove up the road, it was surprising how much furniture that old apron could dust in a matter of seconds. When dinner was ready, Grandma walked out onto the porch, waved her apron, and the men knew it was time to come in from the fields to dinner.

It will be a long time before someone invents something that will replace that "old-time apron" that served so many purposes.[102] They will never be as good as grandma's apron but, when it comes to Long Term Care, hybrid policies can help.

# Section 8

# CONCLUSION

*Chapter 24*

# FISHING FOR WISDOM

I love to fish. When I was a little boy (5 years-old) I couldn't wait to go trout fishing. My dad was an avid fisherman so from a very young age I began looking forward to the day I could join him on the adventure. Every year I waited to be "big enough" to hear my dad say, "Son, its time. Get your gear and let's go catch some fish." It was worse than the anticipation of Christmas Eve having to pretend to be asleep until sunrise. I was proud of my dad and it was the highlight of my life up until that point. I was about to go fishing with my dad!

I remember that day like it was yesterday. The sun was bigger than I could ever remember. My mom told me I was going fishing with my dad until lunch time. He would then bring me home to eat and take a nap. She told me I would want to take a nap afterwards because I was going to be so tired from a big morning of fishing. In reality, I was going to take a nap so my dad could go back out and do some serious fishing! I was so excited that day I kept asking my mom, "When is dad going to wake up so we can go catch our trout?"

Little did I know that going fishing would prove to be one of the most important activities of my young life. Not because of the fish we caught but because of where we went to catch those fish. In my home town lived a man named "Mr. Wise." I thought he was the oldest man I had ever seen. I was 12 and I thought he was probably 99 years old. In fact, he probably was in his nineties and was the oldest person I knew.

I liked him, though, because he had a man-made pond on his

226

property and it was stocked with fish! The deal was you had to ask him for permission to fish before you could go down to the pond. He always said, "Yes," but you couldn't fish until you asked him and spent time talking with him.

He was one the original settlers of this part of the country so he had lots of stories to tell. He shared tales of Indians. He told me about the well on our property that was once the location of the local school house because it had the best water around. He even told me stories of Orville and Wilbur Wright. I am not sure if he actually met them or if he just heard stories about them as he ran his bicycle shop but I found the stores spell-binding.

I was fascinated and frustrated at the same time. I loved hearing his stories but he would often use up my time for fishing. I was allowed to go Mr. Wise's lake often but I had to finish my chores first. Those chores often included cutting the grass around the fence posts with handheld shears or a sickle, or hunting squirrels, rabbits and pheasants for dinner.

When I finished them, mom would let me go with one condition. "Mark, you can fish until the lightning bugs come out."

More times than not, Mr. Wise would talk and talk until he felt I had heard enough. He would then release me to go fishing. By the time I got to the pond, the lightning bugs would begin blinking their neon message with rhythmic regularity, "Mark, go home. Mark, go home." Despite the beauty of the flying lights, my first thoughts would always be, Why did he have to talk so much? Why did he repeat himself so much? I have already heard many of these stories but he had to tell me again.

One day I walked up to the porch like every other fishing day. But this day I could see there was something different about him. His posture and demeanor were obviously sad. It was one of those, "this is not a good time to talk to dad" moments. He was unusually reflective and somber. There were actually tears welling up in his eyes.

I remember his pointer finger reaching out as I came closer. He latched onto my belt and pulled me close until we were eye to eye with one another. Even though I had grown to trust him, it made me uncomfortable. I became aware of details I had never noticed before. His eyes were red around his eye lids. His teeth were not very white and were not evenly spaced. The hair in his ears and nose were way overdue for trimming. I could feel his hand quivering as he held my belt buckle. I could smell his breath and the sweat of the day.

Then I felt an outpouring of sharing that was beyond anything he had ever spoken before. His words startled me. "I wish I was you!" Then he let me go.

I didn't understand. He was the man with the big property. He saw Indians and had a shed full of old, antique bicycles. He knew the Wright brothers. He owned his own pond and it was stocked with fish! He was the most amazing man I had ever met and he wanted to be me.

What could I possibly have that Mr. Wise wanted?

My amazement was interrupted by his next statement, "because if I knew what I know now and was your age I would be wiser." Mr. Wise knew if you could put an old head on young shoulders you would be wiser. If we could somehow mix together the energy of youth with the wisdom of age, we would make remarkable decisions.

It was a life changing moment for me. Prior to this moment, I had been so intent on catching fish I failed to realize that an even bigger catch was within my grasp. If I wanted, I could become wiser than Mr. Wise! All I had to do was listen and learn.

I still loved fishing but I became more patient with his stories. I decided it was in my best interest to expand my list of sources. So, I started asking questions of others I considered wiser than me. I interviewed older folks to find out what they knew. I hung out with some of the local preachers in my area and began taking notes on their sermons. I even began counting how many times they used hand gestures in their messages and which hand motions strengthened their points.

I would like to tell you that I have always followed the wisdom I discovered but you would know that it is not true because no one has ever applied everything they have learned. That doesn't mean we should stop learning from each other and trying to learn from the experience of others.

## Borrow from my Experience

Many people have learned the hard way and one of my hopes is that I can help many of us avoid some of the typical mistakes people make with misplaced confidence. For instance, I have heard all of the following statements:

*I'll burn my house down before the government gets it.*

*I'll just hide my money in a can in the back yard. That way nobody but my family will get any of it.*

*I'll give the house away before I die.*

*I'm not going to report any cash money I receive. There won't be any tax liability that way.*

*I'll put my money in someone's else's name to collect benefits.*

*We'll live together and not remarry so we can retain our benefits.*

*I would never let my mom go to a nursing home.*

*I don't need a durable power of attorney or living will because my family won't put me on life support.*

*Just dig a hole and put me in it. I don't need to spend all that money on a funeral. (Justification for no burial plot and a paid up 2,000 life insurance policy they bought when the insurance agent came to the door.)*

*My family knows who gets what. It won't be my problem because I will be dead. Let them worry about it and fight over it if they want.*

*Don't worry about the bills. When I'm dead what are they going to do about it?*

*I'll just live with my kids.*

*I don't need other people's advice. My kids are smart. They are doctors, lawyers or run their own business. They all have degrees so I don't have to worry.*

*I don't have enough to worry about. As a result, I don't really need a trust.*

*I left the house to my wife. She can sell it and then move into a smaller place. What is left over should be enough money for her to live on.*

*My family won't argue about stuff when I die. They love each other!*

## Words of Wisdom

Listening to others who had more life experience than I did taught me some very important lessons in life.

Good information leads to good decisions. You can't make good choices based on what you don't know. You need information that is relevant and reliable in order to build confidence in the plan you are assembling for your finances.

Mistakes make you smarter. I don't say this to encourage you to make mistakes. I simply say it so that you won't be afraid of mistakes. Anyone who has ever experienced significant success will tell you not to be afraid of failure. For example:

*"Failure isn't fatal, but failure to change might be." – John Wooden*

*"Only those who dare to fail greatly can ever achieve greatly." - Robert F. Kennedy*

*"The phoenix must burn to emerge."* - *Janet Fitch*

*"Success is stumbling from failure to failure with no loss of enthusiasm."* - *Winston Churchill* [103]

These people all see failure as the gateway to success because every setback or misstep gives you wisdom for future decisions, if you are willing to learn from them. As I look back on my journey, I can say with full confidence that some of the insight I treasure most today was acquired through experiences that were painful. For instance:

I learned to understand contracts by being robbed blind in a construction contract. I was angry at the time but look back on it with gratitude because of how it sharpened my senses.

I learned to think like a businessman when another business owner tried to take over my business. I saw him as an adversary at first but over time I was willing to accept that his actions made me smarter.

I learned the real value of a family estate from a lady who slapped me on the back of the head. Really! I was meeting with a couple in their home talking about estate planning. As I reviewed their bank accounts, investments and retirement accounts, I came up with a number that represented their assets. When I announced the number to the couple, the wife reached up and slapped me on the back of my head. I felt just like Tony DiNozzo on the show NCIS being slapped by Jethro Gibbs. She didn't say anything, she just slapped me. I took another look at the numbers thinking I must have made a mistake. When I realized I had accounted for everything correctly, I announced the same number again only to be met with another slap on the back of my head. This time, I turned toward her and asked, "What? I know the numbers are right."

Without hesitation she responded, "This home is where our family memories were made. My kids and grandkids know they can always come home here and find a place of safety and love. Our family built our name and reputation on this property. That is worth a lot more than what you wrote down on that paper of yours."

I learned the value of waiting from a missionary. We were working on a project together and he accidently nicked my leg with a chain saw. It sounds worse than it was as it was a minor cut that could, of course, been a major injury. Recovering from that accident forced me to sit still longer than I ever had in my life. At first it was agonizing but after a couple of days I began to see the value of being able to sit quietly and wait for circumstances to line up.

I learned the importance of finishing what you start from a foreman who had trouble finishing and communicated poorly. As a result, we had a hard time finishing anything. It bothered me enough to engrave the thought the job is not over until it is over.

**Some people will inspire you, remember them.**
It is easy to become cynical about people if you focus on the individuals in life who have done you wrong. We have all been surprised by the unscrupulous or unskilled actions of others. At the same time, we all know people of remarkable actions who have proved to be good role models. The choice to remember the inspirational more than the cynical will give you peace and strength. Some of the most inspirational people on the path of my life are:

*Donne Benedict.* Donne was an elderly client of mine who

brightened my day every time I saw her. She always put on bright red lipstick and prepped her hair before I showed up. Many of you may think of a traitor named Benedict Arnold when you hear her name but what I hear is one of the most honorable names in my history. She always sat on the same bench in the corner of her dining room when I visited. She always insisted on affectionately greeting me which, of course, would leave a big set of red lips on my cheeks.

Early on, I helped her husband with their investments. The money then passed to Donne. I helped her set up a plan in which she had confidence and in which we were both pleased. But then a broker who had previously helped them convinced her to put the money back into the stock market. For many people it would have been a good move but at her age it was too volatile. She consistently watched her money go up and down. It made her nervous but she had a hard time admitting she had made a mistake. It apparently was easier to say that I was wrong than to admit that she had made a mistake.

I found out that one of her children was on disability so I paid her a visit. She courageously told me how she had moved her funds but now wanted to make a change back. Having a child on disability presented its own unique challenges so that needed to be addressed also. We settled her money and then set up a special needs trust.

When cancer finally caught up with her, I was able to visit her in the hospital. Her courage in admitting she needed help had allowed us to set up a sound set of tools that provided for her disabled son and kept the money in the family. The trust enabled her son and daughter to settle her estate without fighting and utilize the funds to set them both up for retirement. Her courage turned into a real legacy for her family.

In gratitude for the help she received, she used to say that I was an angel sent to bring hope in the midst of a difficult situation. Her gratitude and humility still inspire me today.

*The traveling nurse.* Monica is one of the smartest and most compassionate people I have ever met. She was a traveling nurse who specialized in assisting with open heart surgery. She was an intellectual from Louisiana with a loud, cackling laugh. It was quite the combination. Most of the time, she was the smartest person in the room but she always carried herself in a humble manner and was willing to let the others of us in the room act like the experts.

She was amused by my caveman abilities even though she was way more sophisticated and educated than I was. Her approach to life was completely different than mine and sometimes it was better! As a result, there are times in my life, even today, when I ask myself, "What would Monica do right now?" She taught me that there is a time to be Superman and a time to be Clark Kent. So, at times, I need a Mark decision and I rely on my instincts. Other times, I need a Monica decision (more humble and gentle), so I rely on her example. There have been many times in my life where I did better because I humbly did things her way.

*Vic – A Symbol of Victory.* Every once in a while you meet someone who responds to life the way you hope you will. Vic is one such man in my experience. I met him because of Mimi, a longtime client who has become a friend. We have laughed together, cried together and solved problems together. She has become a sort of second mom who even ends our phone calls with an affectionate, "I love you."

Vic and Mimi are amazing to me because of how they have responded to the adversity in their lives. Mimi's first husband died and she assumed she would probably spend the rest of her life alone. Vic, likewise, had lost two previous wives to terminal illnesses. When they found each other their interests and their common pain created a strong bond.

I was thrilled when Mimi called and, with an obvious glow in her voice, announced, "I think I have fallen in love." I was equally stunned when she shared the news that the new love of her life had been diagnosed with cancer during their engagement.

I half expected them to cancel the wedding in a mutual decision that "it was just too much." Instead, they marched forward with their wedding plans and modified their honeymoon itinerary. They originally were planning on a cruise immediately after the wedding but instead took Vic to the hospital after their wedding ceremony so he could get his regularly scheduled treatment.

I visited them a few months after the wedding anticipating the mood would be somber, maybe even pathetic. Instead, I was greeted by a vibrant couple who were laughing together, teasing one another and telling stories about how good their life was as a couple.

I couldn't help but ask, "Vic, how do you summon the courage to be positive in the face of cancer after losing two wives to a terminal illness?"

He looked me straight in the eyes and said, "You have to stay positive, my friend. I didn't do so well with my first wife. I got negative and angry with life for way too long. I finally came around and was able to be supportive of her but it was tough. When my second wife was diagnosed I told her, 'We have to stay positive or the medicine won't do its job. The doctors need to treat your body but we need to treat your heart.' It was difficult but some of my sweetest memories in life came from our ability to stay positive in the midst of the battle. Mimi and I decided we are going to make the most of the time we have rather than spend the time complaining over things we have no control over anyway. Besides, have you seen her. She is really pretty when she dawns that big smile!"

As he talked it hit me that I complained more about the toothache I had last year than Vic ever will about having cancer. In the face of his weakness I knew I had become a stronger person that day.

*Max, my martial arts instructor in Africa.* His job description was focused on teaching us combative skills but his real goal was to teach us how to perform well under stress. In the midst of intense training when we wanted to give in and give up, he would remind us that the sky is still blue and the grass is still green. In the stress of the moment, all we could see was red and he knew it would eventually ruin us. I am a better man today because I learned to see blue and green!

*My warrant officer in the Navy.* I liked her even though most of the guys in the unit didn't because she was never satisfied. They thought it was ridiculous that we had to learn how to insert an IV while we were upside down using our "off hand." Since I am right-handed, that meant I had to do this all with my left hand. She announced that we were not good enough for her team if we could not accomplish this feat. She taught me that I am capable of more than I realized and more than I would have considered on my own.

*Marge, the dancing FBI agent.* I met Marge through my part-time pursuit of ballroom dancing. She danced with me for years and we did well together. One day, I put in a different CD that randomly played a waltz. Right in front of me, she transformed. She got taller as her posture straightened. She started humming and singing as she came alive in my arms. For a moment in time she was a young lady once again. When the music stopped she whispered, "That was my and my husband's song. Thank you."

Her usual routine was to book her next lesson before she left the studio but not this time. Instead she softly said, "I am going to visit my husband."

The next day I received a call from her family. "Marge passed away last night. Thank you so much for dancing with her. It kept the memory of our dad alive and helped her feel young."

Anytime I think of the power of love to energize our lives and build deep memories I think of Marge.

*Peter, the man who taught me how to finish well.* We worked together for an entire day to record life insurance policies, make sure taxes were in order and bills were paid. He knew he was getting close to the end of his life and wanted to cover his bases. We also talked about him writing a "love letter" to his family which he wanted to have read at his funeral.

This is something I recommend to all my clients. It gives people an opportunity to say what may be hard to say in person and adds human capital to the asset distribution. I encourage people to ask:

- What would you like to say to your wife and children?
- What advice would you like to give to the people you love the most?
- How do you want them to respond at your funeral?
- How do you want them to handle the family events (holidays, birthdays, weddings, etc.) that will happen during the next year?

(You can find a worksheet for this letter on my website – see the back of the book for the address)

When the business is done, I then shut the book and read the letter to the family. It brings closure and moves the focus back to the relationships rather than the money. It gives permission to the family to grieve appropriately and move on with life in a natural way. I love this process because it causes the last things that are said to be the most important things.

As I was finishing up with Peter, He asked me, "Is everything in order? Have we covered everything?"

I responded, "From a legal and financial perspective, we have taken care of everything. The only thing that is not done is that letter you said you want to write."

I told him I had some paperwork to do which I was going to take care of in my car before I left. It took me a little while so it was quite late when I finally pulled out of the driveway. A mile down the road my phone rang.

Peter's wife asked, "How far down the road are you?"

"Not far," I said, "I am just about a mile away."

It felt a little odd so I started thinking, I bet I left my briefcase or something else at their house. It is nice of them to call.

Before I could ask, she interjected, "Can you come back to the house?"

I could tell from the tone in her voice that I needed to go back. As I walked in the room I saw Peter sitting still in his chair. It was obvious that he was no longer with us but my attention was drawn to him. As I approached him I noticed he was holding on to the love letter he had just finished for his loved ones.

Peter had built his financial fences well. He had taken care of his money and taken care of his family. Most importantly, he had spoken to the hearts of the people he cared about the most. His example gave me a new goal.

I hope my last act on earth is a treasured memory my family will carry for the rest of their lives. As you plan your journey and build your financial fences, it is my goal that your story will be a treasured memory as well.

# ENDNOTES

### Section 1: Income Planning

## Chapter 3: Laugh At The Future

1. http://www.helpguide.org/life/humor_laughter_health.htm
2. http://fidonet.ozzmosis.com/echomail.php/diabetes/963bbb1f7fe7a1a4.html
3. http://www.retirement-cafe.com/Retirement-Planning.html
4. http://www.retirement-cafe.com/Saving-for-Retirement.html
5. http://www.anecdotage.com/index.php?aid=19043. [Sources: Biography magazine, July 2003, p. 23; Economist, Oct 21st 2004]

## Chapter 4: Identify Your Income

6. http://www.thejoyofbeingretired.com/Funny-Retirement-Quotes-and-Sayings.html
7. http://www.history.com/this-day-in-history/fdr-signs-social-security-act
8. http://www.guy-sports.com/funny/funny_senior_moments.htm
9. Source: Calculations by the Center for Retirement Research at Boston College, based on the U.S. Census Bureau 2009 Current Population Survey http://www.retirement-cafe.com/Retirement-Income.html
10. 2014 Retirement Confidence Survey, Employee Benefit Research Institute, http://www.ebri.org/pdf/surveys/rcs/2014/RCS14.FS-1.Conf.Final.pdf. The 55% figure includes 18% who are very confident and 37% who are somewhat confident.
11. http://www.brainyquote.com/quotes/quotes/b/brucelee383809.html
12. http://www.quotegarden.com/goals.html
13. http://www.inspirational-quotes.info/goals1.html
14. http://www.nytimes.com/2012/11/29/business/zig-ziglar-86-motivational-speaker-and-author.html?_r=0
15. http://academictips.org/blogs/funny-short-stories/

## Chapter 5: In Sync With Inflation

16. http://www.guy-sports.com/jokes/retirement_jokes.htm
17. For information about "Deflategate," see http://nypost.com/tag/deflategate/; http://www.si.com/nfl/2015/09/06/roger-goodell-image-after-tom-brady-deflategate-appeal-ruling; http://www.nationalreview.com/article/423638/goodell-brady-deflategate-mess
18. http://inflationdata.com/inflation/inflation/DecadeInflation.asp
19. http://www.bls.gov/opub/ted/2012/ted_20120302.htm
20. The Lifetime Distribution of Health Care Costs by Berhanu Alemayehu and Kenneth E. Warner. Health Services Research, June 2004, http://www.ncbi.nlm.nih.gov/pmc/articles/PMC1361028/, p. 11.
21. Health of Americans 65 and Older: How States Stack Up, USA Today, May 26, 2013, http://www.usatoday.com/story/news/nation/2013/05/28/senior-citizens-health-care-report/2354635/. You can read the current United Health Foundation Senior Report at http://cdnfiles.americashealthrankings.org/SiteFiles/Reports/AHR-Senior-Report-2014.pdf
22. http://www.yuksrus.com/taxman.html

## Chapter 6: Execute Your Plan

23. Numbers are based on CPS 2013 Annual Social and Economic Supplement, 2012 Family Income, Table All Primary Families, All Races, http://www.census.gov/hhes/www/cpstables/032013/faminc/finc02_000.htm.

### Section 2: You and Your Home

## Chapter 7: Property and Casualty Coverage

24. Let go of your Stresses! http://academictips.org/blogs/let-go-of-your-stresses/
25. The Beginner's Guide To Homeowners' Insurance, By Marcy Tolkoff, http://www.investopedia.com/articles/pf/08/homeowner-insurance.asp?rp=i
26. The Beginner's Guide To Homeowners' Insurance, By Marcy Tolkoff, http://www.investopedia.com/articles/pf/08/homeowner-insurance.asp?rp=i
27. The Beginner's Guide To Homeowners' Insurance, By Marcy Tolkoff, http://www.investopedia.com/articles/pf/08/homeowner-insurance.asp?rp=i

## Chapter 8: Consider a Public Adjuster

28. http://www.guy-sports.com/humor/sports/sports_golf.htm
29. http://www.goodreads.com/work/quotes/22371540.
30. Adapted from Public Adjuster Representation in Citizens Property Insurance Corporation Claims Extend the Time to Reach a Settlement and Also Increases Payments to Citizens' Policyholder, Office of Program Policy Analysis and Government Accountability, January 2010, Report No. 10-06. http://www.oppaga.state.fl.us/MonitorDocs/Reports/pdf/1006rpt.pdf. P. 10.

## Chapter 9: Revokable Living Trusts

31. http://www.nolo.com/legal-encyclopedia/revocable-living-trusts.html
32. Adapted from http://www.nolo.com/legal-encyclopedia/revocable-living-trusts.html
33. "Three Documents You Shouldn't Do Without," By George D. Lambert. http://www.investopedia.com/articles/pf/05/050905.asp

# Section 3: Types of Investors

## Chapter 10: Your Investor Style

34. http://www.brainyquote.com/quotes/authors/a/ayn_rand.html
35. http://www.brainyquote.com/quotes/authors/r/ronald_reagan.html
36. Buy American. I Am by Warren Buffett, http://www.nytimes.com/2008/10/17/opinion/17buffett.html?_r=0
37. Information on railways was found at Railroads, Dictionary of American History, 2003 - http://www.encyclopedia.com/topic/Railroads.aspx and Horse's Pass - http://www.snopes.com/history/american/gauge.asp

## Chapter 11: The WINDS that Blow

38. http://www.pinterest.com/explore/funny-monday-quotes/
39. http://www.pinterest.com/explore/funny-monday-quotes/
40. http://www.pinterest.com/explore/funny-monday-quotes/
41. Athletes, Luck, and Superstition on St. Patrick's Day by Clay Davis. http://www.foxsports.com/college-football/outkick-the-coverage/athletes-luck-and-superstition-on-st-patricks-day-031712
42. Being Amused by Apophenia: Can we find pleasure and amusement in faulty reasoning? by Bruce Poulsen, PhD. Published July 31, 2012. http://www.psychologytoday.com/blog/reality-play/201207/being-amused-apophenia
43. http://money.howstuffworks.com/ponzi-scheme5.htm

## Chapter 12: Changing How the WINDS Blow

44. http://www.changestartswithme.org/character_traits.php
45. http://academictips.org/blogs/improving-self-confidence/
46. http://www.rajeshsetty.com/2007/01/24/a-story-on-problem-solving-contributed-by-sridhar-krishnan/

# Section 4: Healthcare

## Chapter 13: A Plan that Matches You

47. http://www.aarp.org/personal-growth/transitions/boomers_65/

48. Needed Savings for Health Care in Retirement Continue to Fall, ebri.org, October 28, 2014, http://www.ebri.org/pdf/PR1097.HlthSvgs.28Oct14.pdf
49. Fidelity Estimates Couples Retiring in 2013 Will Need $220,000 to Pay Medical Expenses Throughout Retirement, http://www.fidelity.com/inside-fidelity/individual-investing/fidelity-estimates-couples-retiring-in-2013-will-need-220000-to-pay-medical-expenses-throughout-retirement.
50. How to pay for health care in retirement by Robert Powell, USA Today, November 1, 2014. http://usat.ly/1wRwSux refers to http://kff.org/medicare/issuebrief/healthcareonabudgetthefinancialburdenofhealthspendingbymedicarehouseholds/

## Section 5: Life Insurance

### Chapter 14: Life Insurance is like a Tractor

51. Tractors by Chris Woodford, http://www.explainthatstuff.com/tractors.html
52. Tractors: An Introduction, http://www.agriculturalproductsindia.com/agricultural-machinery-equipments/agricultural-machinery-equipments-tractor.html
53. What are farm tractors used for? https://answers.yahoo.com/question/index-?qid=20080219222728AAzBhT5
54. Tractor Implements by Curtis Von Fange, http://www.yesterdaystractors.com/articles/artint210.htm
55. Tractors by Chris Woodford, http://www.explainthatstuff.com/tractors.html
56. Tractor Quotes. This quote is from Les Claypool. http://www.brainyquote.com/quotes/quotes/l/lesclaypoo596208.html?src=t_tractor
57. A response from Alex to Farm & Farmers Quotes, http://www.quotesquotations.com/funny/farm-farmers-quotes.htm
58. Tractors: An Introduction, http://www.agriculturalproductsindia.com/agricultural-machinery-equipments/agricultural-machinery-equipments-tractor.html
59. Adapted from Tractor Implements by Curtis Von Fange, http://www.yesterdaystractors.com/articles/artint210.htm
60. http://www.qualityininsurance.com/humour.htm
61. http://www.qualityininsurance.com/humour.htm
62. http://www.qualityininsurance.com/humour.htm
63. http://www.oxymoronlist.com/category/oxymoron-quotes/page/3/
64. http://www.oxymoronlist.com/category/oxymoron-quotes/page/3/
65. http://www.oxymoronlist.com/category/oxymoron-quotes/page/4/
66. http://www.funny.com/cgi-bin/WebObjects/Funny.woa/wa/funny?fn=CMTXE
67. http://pages.citebite.com/c2y6l3p2t8uga and http://www.asa.org/policy/resources/stats/
68. https://www.debt.org/students/debt/
69. http://www.huffingtonpost.com/kyle-mccarthy/10-fun-facts-about-student-loan-debt_b_4639044.html
70. 10 Fun Facts About the Student Debt Crisis, by Kyle McCarthy.January 22, 2014. http://www.huffingtonpost.com/kyle-mccarthy/10-fun-facts-about-student-loan-debt_b_4639044.html

### Chapter 15: Selections that Work for You

71. http://www.qualityininsurance.com/humour.htm
72. http://www.barricksinsurance.com/insurance_jokes.html

### Chapter 16: Surprising Solutions

73. 6 Famous Brands Started or Saved by Life Insurance, http://www.lifehealthpro.com/2012/04/06/6-famous-brands-started-or-saved-by-life-insurance?t=employee-benefits&page=4.
74. http://www.designingdisney.com/content/construction-disneyland

## Section 6: Annuities

### Chapter 17: The Origins of Annuities

75. Do as the Romans did — with annuities by Stan Haithcock. http://www.marketwatch. com/story/do-as-the-romans-did-with-annuities-2013-06-04?pagenumber=1.
76. The Story of Annuities, The Backbone of Retirement Throughout the History of the World, http://www.advisorsfirst.net/media/DIR_104/DIR_16601/d3991cb04c55ce-faffff80ddffffd523.pdf.
77. The Story of Annuities, The Backbone of Retirement Throughout the History of the World, http://www.advisorsfirst.net/media/DIR_104/DIR_16601/d3991cb04c55ce-faffff80ddffffd523.pdf.

## Chapter 18: Annuities in America

78. Keown, Arthur J, John D. Martin, J. William Petty, and David F. Scott, Jr., Founda-tions of Finance: The Logic and Practice of Financial Management: Prentice Hall. 2003, Chapter 5, The Time Value of Money, p. 135.
79. Benjamin Franklin's Legacy, http://www.bfit.edu/The-College/About-the-College/Benjamin-Franklin-s-Legacy.
80. Top 10 Civil War Innovations, http://news.discovery.com/history/us-history/civ-il-war-innovations-110328.htm.

## Chapter 19: New Options for a Chaging World

81. 10 Jobs That Didn't Exist 10 Years Ago by Meghan Casserly, http://www.forbes.com/sites/meghancasserly/2012/05/11/10-jobs-that-didnt-exist-10-years-ago/.
82. Retirement in America will never be the same. https://www.allianzlife.com/retire-ment-and-planning-tools/reclaiming-the-future/white-paper-findings.
83. A Short Lesson in Bad Decision-Making by Adam Taggert, http://www.peakprosperi-ty.com/blog/80482/short-lesson-bad-decisionmaking.
84. Information and quotes on The Death Road were drawn from "The Death Road!" by Andrew Morgan, http://teacherontwowheels.com/2008/09/30/the-death-road/; "Cycling the World's Most Dangerous Road," http://comedytravelwriting. com/2013/05/19/cycling-the-worlds-most-dangerous-road/; "A 15,000ft descent, sheer drops and 300 deaths a year: Welcome to Bolivia's Death Road, the terrifying route tourists love to cycle," by Michael Gadd, http://www.dailymail.co.uk/travel/article-2729754/A-15-000ft-descent-sheer-drops-300-deaths-year-Welcome-Bolivia-s-Death-Road-terrifying-route-tourists-love-cycle.html#ixzz3JTDvGMlB.

## Section 7: Long Term Care

## Chapter 20: It's Personal

85. http://data.worldbank.org/country/united-states
86. http://www.efmoody.com/estate/lifeexpectancy.html
87. These stats found in 40 Must-Know Statistics About Long-Term Care by Christine Benz. 08/09/2012. http://news.morningstar.com/articlenet/article.aspx?id=564139.
88. https://www.genworth.com/lats-talk/ltc/planning-for-long-term-care/statistics.html
89. https://www.genworth.com/lats-talk/ltc/planning-for-long-term-care/statistics.html
90. Long Term Care Statistics, www.ltctree.com/long-term-care-statistics/
91. http://www.history.com/topics/baby-boomers
92. Long Term Care Statistics, www.ltctree.com/long-term-care-statistics/
93. Long Term Care Statistics, www.ltctree.com/long-term-care-statistics/
94. http://www.suddenlysenior.com/HURrICNEPREPARATION.html

## Chapter 21: What Is It?

95. www.Genworth.com/costofcare

## Chapter 22: Climb the H.I.L.L. Together

96. These responses are based on information presented by Genworth in Let's Talk: Con-versations that make a difference, 08/03/2012, https://www.genworth.com/dam/Amer-icas/US/PDFs/Consumer/Product/LTC/113025WEB.pdf
97. http://www.butlerwebs.com/jokes/babyboomer2.htm

## Chapter 23: Hybrids Can Help

98. Commercial Banana Plants are Perfect Clones of One Another by Daven Hiskey, http://www.todayifoundout.com/index.php/2010/06/commercial-banana-plants-are-perfect-clones-of-one-another/
99. http://www.nutsforalmonds.com/history.htm
100. How Hybrids Work, http://www.fueleconomy.gov/feg/hybridtech.shtml.
101. How Hybrid Cars Work, http://www.howstuffworks.com/hybrid-car.htm
102. http://www.suddenlysenior.com/grandmasapron.html

## Section 8: Conclusion

## Chapter 24: Fishing for Wisdom

103. 30 Powerful Quotes on Failure by Ekaterina Walter. http://www.forbes.com/sites/ekaterinawalter/2013/12/30/30-powerful-quotes-on-failure/

To contact Mark
or to find more resources
for building your financial fences

www.buildingfinancialfences.com

39626173R10138

Made in the USA
Middletown, DE
21 January 2017